JAPANESE
MOTIFS
FOR

NEEDLEPOINT

JAPANESE MOTIFS FOR

NEEDLEPOINT

By Sally Nicoletti

Photographs by Joseph Nicoletti

WILLIAM MORROW & COMPANY, INC.   NEW YORK

*To Desneige Bernier,
dear friend,
in loving memory of Roland*

PRINTED IN THE UNITED STATES OF AMERICA

Book design by Sallie Baldwin,
ANTLER & BALDWIN, INC.

Contents

Introduction

The needlepoint designs in this book are based on a source that has not been used for this purpose before—the motifs found in Japanese Nō theater costumes, which I first saw at an exhibition of such costumes held at Japan House in New York City in the summer of 1977. The woven and embroidered silks of which the costumes are made revealed exciting design structures and color harmonies that were new to me and proved easily adaptable to needlepoint.

Intended as they were for fabrics to be made into garments, the designs are usually composed of large repeated motifs, the arrangement of the colors varying within each, often laid on a continuous geometric ground pattern. Although most of the projects in this collection feature isolated motifs, many of these can easily be repeated for larger projects.

Because of the importance of the costume in a Nō play, its motifs often suggesting the qualities of the personage being portrayed, some of the designs, by their general angularity and intensity of color, may suggest boldness and action, while others, by their more sinuous contours and subdued coloring, may suggest contemplation. Actually you will find that each design subtly combines both elements, as well as other pairs of opposite qualities, in varying proportions and with harmonious results.

The Nō theater has its roots in medieval courtly elegance, politics, history, Zen Buddhism, and, ultimately, indigenous Shinto custom, which it shares with the other two Japanese theater traditions, the doll theater and Kabuki.[1] The Nō is distinguished for having preserved, through a number of stylistic and political eras, the aesthetic ideals of suggestion and evocation so admired by its early patrons, the feudal aristocracy.

Therefore, tradition dictates that the Nō stage be austere; its few props may be as simple as autumn grasses beside the suggestion of a well.[2] The recitation and movements of the principal actor, *shite*, and secondary actor, *waki*, are very slow and ponderous, conforming to established conventions of mime and gesture,[3] as are the music of the orchestra and the chanting of the chorus. The cumulative effect is one of solemnity, timelessness, and unreality, in keeping with the tragic theme of most Nō plays.

The costume of the *shite* is important in the creation of this mood.[4] Besides the information it conveys by its sumptuousness as to the prominence of the *shite*, its design may suggest qualities of character, youth or age, masculinity or femininity and may refer to a particular time of the year as well.[5,6,7] The costume may even be used in the action to serve the purposes of the play.[8]

The repertory of the Nō theater is said to consist of between 230 and 250 plays, established in large part during its early period. There are five principal Nō companies or schools: *Kwanze*, *Komparu*, *Hōshō*, *Kongō*, and *Kita*. The plots are derived from a variety of native and foreign sources, mythical and legendary, fantastic, historical, and contemporary. A number of the plays were inspired by classical Japanese literature such as the *Ise Monogatori* (ninth century), the *Yamato Monogatori* (tenth century), and the *Genji Monogatori* (eleventh century), as well as the collection of Indian, Chinese, and Japanese tales and legends known as the *Konjaku Monogatori* (twelfth century).[9]

The traditional format of a program of Nō included five plays, one from each category—briefly: (1.) God Nō, (2.) Warrior Nō, (3.) Woman Nō, (4.) Miscellaneous Nō, and (5.) Demon Nō—alternating with *Kyogen* (comic interludes). A contemporary program, however, would usually feature only three Nō plays with *Kyogen*.

I hope you will enjoy this book and find the directions and graphs clear and easy to follow. If you are an advanced needlepointer, you might want to use these designs in planning special projects of your own. If you're just looking into needlepoint, I hope they lead you to auspicious beginnings.

SALLY NICOLETTI

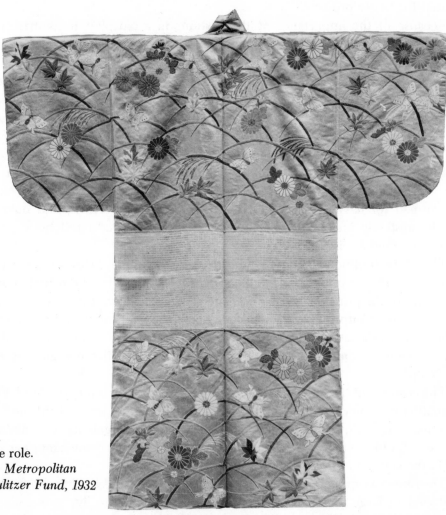

Nō robe for female role.
—*Courtesy of The Metropolitan Museum of Art, Pulitzer Fund, 1932*

THE BASICS

CANVAS

This is available in a number of gauges (number of mesh—threads of canvas—per inch) and in three basic types:

> Plain mono canvas—single woven threads,
> Interlocked mono canvas—intertwined double threads that are locked where they mesh, and
> Penelope canvas—double threads interlocking at the mesh, but open so that the small spaces in between can be worked in petit point (which is not dealt with in this book).

The most important consideration in the choice of canvas is quality. Look for imported cotton canvas; Zweigart is the most widely available high-quality canvas, and it is distinguished by the orange threads woven into its selvage edges. Interlocked canvas is most suitable for articles that will get little or no wear, such as wall hangings and purely ornamental cushions. For all upholstered pieces it's best to use plain mono or penelope canvas. Not only are they stronger canvases, especially the penelope, but it is thought that the slightly rougher surface of interlocked canvas may have an abrasive effect on the yarn over time.

To Prepare the Canvas:

Secure the raw edges with ¾- or 1-inch-wide masking tape, or trim the corners of the canvas and apply double-fold bias tape all around with a sewing machine. Always mark "top" along the upper edge of the canvas in order to maintain your orientation in relation to the graph.

For all the designs in this book, the small squares on the graphs represent the crossed *mesh* of canvas to be covered by yarn stitches, the colors of which are designated by numbers and symbols. Especially for designs given in four quarter graphs, it will be helpful first to find the center of your canvas. If the center of the graph for the design falls on a *mesh* of canvas (a square on the graph), then mark the mesh of your canvas closest to its center with a hard pencil or Nepō needlework marker. If the center of the design falls *between* mesh (a line on the graph), this is actually in the center *hole* of your canvas; mark the horizontal and vertical grooves intersecting in this hole. If you find it most comfortable to work from the center out, start here and work parts of each quarter as you go. If you prefer to begin at the upper-right-hand corner and work across and down, ending at the lower-left-hand corner, then generally begin at a point an inch from both the top and right edges of the canvas.

Exceptions to this rule are wall hangings and upholstered pieces that may need extra canvas margin for mounting or adding work for fitting. Another exception occurs in cases such as numbers 21, 22, and 23, which are rectangular pieces set on the diagonal, worked mainly in Basic Stitch. If they are worked without a frame, they will surely become very distorted; therefore, 2 inches of canvas margin are allowed all around, rather than one, so that on completion each can be cut out, following mesh an inch from the work diagonally, and then rebound as rectangles and blocked. (Oval pieces set on the diagonal but worked mainly in compensating stitches, such as numbers 24, 25, and 26, may be blocked as they are, following the lines of the square in which they are enclosed.)

Round pieces or oval pieces to be worked with their axes in the usual vertical and horizontal orientation should be worked within marked rectangles or squares (given as dotted lines in the graphs) and blocked as such. Diagonals marked from their corners also help establish the design.

Using a Stitchery Frame:

You may find this most helpful, especially when working graphed designs. The Quandra frame pictured here, from Pandora Products, allows the use of both hands, comes with two sizes of horizontal bars, and adjusts for use in a chair, on a table, in bed, and even in a car. The top and bottom edges of the canvas to be

worked are basted to the tapes of the frame's horizontal bars, which are then placed on the vertical bars and tightened to hold the canvas taut. The use of a frame will prevent your canvas from distorting with heavy use of Basic Stitch in your design. If you like to "pluck" stitches, bringing the needle in and out of the canvas in two separate movements, the stitchery frame will free both your hands to make this easier. ("Plucking" is also recommended in general for those who dislike having their canvases become distorted.)

For smallish projects you can make a stitchery frame with canvas stretcher bars, available in art supply and frame shops as well as some needlework shops. You should buy two pairs of bars to coincide with the dimensions of your piece of canvas and staple the unworked margins along the surface of the bars. This frame must be held with one hand or propped against a table, while being supported on your lap, and it is not adjustable in any way.

Blocking:

The most common blocking procedure involves a square or rectangular piece worked in Basic Stitch (Basketweave and/or Continental stitches). The Basketweave Stitch (worked diagonally) distorts the canvas less than the Continental Stitch (worked horizontally). However, to restore a distorted canvas to its original

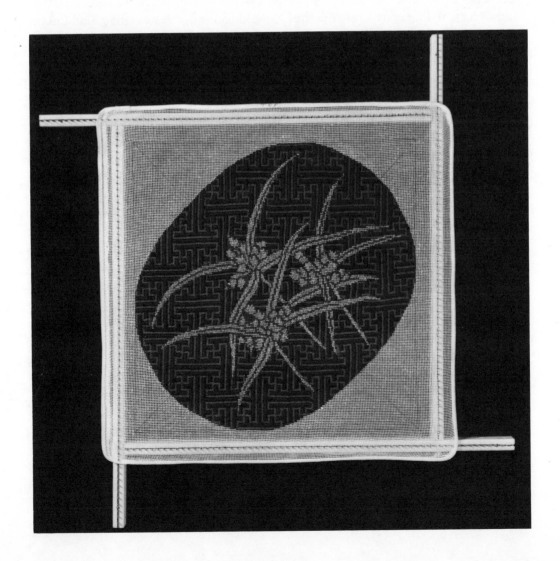

dimensions, have a large wooden board marked (with heavy permanent marker) with a grid of 1-inch squares. Soak a terry towel in cold water, and without wringing it out, roll up your worked canvas in it and let the roll sit overnight so that the canvas is thoroughly dampened the next day. Then line up an edge of the canvas, faceup, along a grid line of your board, which you should be able to see through the canvas margin, and staple or thumbtack it securely. Do this with all four edges, easing and adjusting as you go, until your piece is properly squared off and back to its size and shape.

With a stitchery blocker, such as the one pictured, available from Frank A. Edmunds & Co., all you have to do, after dampening the canvas, is to ease it, edge by edge, onto the teeth along its stretcher bars, after you have adjusted these to the approximate size of your piece. The blocker will accommodate pieces up to 24″ by 24″.

As noted before, odd-shaped pieces, such as ovals and rounds, should be blocked as rectangles and squares. This applies when the piece is on the same axes as your piece of canvas. When the axes of your design are diagonal to those of your canvas, as in designs number 21 through 26, you may have to cut it out, rebind it, and then block it, following its own rectangular outline. Fortunately the only designs in this group that will be so distorted (unless you have worked them on a frame and/or "plucked" the design) that they will require this extra step are numbers 24, 25, and 26. (Extra unworked margin is included in the canvas dimensions given, so that you can cut out the piece along mesh of canvas diagonally, about an inch from the worked edges.)

Finishing:

I feel strongly that finishing needlepoint is best left to an experienced professional. That person, you or someone else, will need from one to four stitches of worked area running along each edge of the piece to be taken under. So this should be taken into consideration when you plan any piece. Many of the designs in this book end exactly on repeated motifs, but wouldn't suffer if ¼ to ⅓ inch were taken under in finishing.

For any cushion up to about 16″ by 16″, half a yard of backing fabric will be sufficient and will allow enough for diagonal strips to be cut and pieced together for piping after the backing piece has been cut out. The most suitable fabrics for backing needlepoint cushions are heavyweight cottons, no-wale corduroys, velvets, and linens; the greater the natural fiber content, the easier it will be to work with and the more supportive it will be for the needlepoint. In no circumstances use a fabric with any stretch to it because a cushion backed with it will not hold its shape and piped edges will be ripply rather than crisp.

Oval and round cushions are best box-finished rather than knife-edge-finished, and the usual inner muslin cushion should be amply stuffed. (All cushions should be rather overstuffed as they will pack down soon enough. A little extra filling tucked into corners will keep them from dog-earing.) A zipper in the back will allow the inner cushion to be removed for flat dry cleaning of the needlepoint case.

Count on upholstered items, such as chairs, footstools, etc., requiring at least an extra inch of worked area to be taken under all around. So, after careful template making, taking the "rise" of the piece into account, add your extra inch all around, and then yet another, just in case. (Perhaps your upholsterer will be especially enthusiastic and wish to build up a fine old piece from the inside in order to restore it to its original Victorian amplitude, thereby increasing the surface area to be covered. It would be wise to consult with him about the outline of your template.)

YARNS

Persian yarn is the generic term for *three-ply wool yarns* that are separable into three threads. When you work in Basic Stitch (see THE STITCHES), the rule of thumb about how many threads to use with which gauge of canvas is: three threads on 10-mesh-per-inch canvas, two threads on 12- to 14-mesh canvas, and one thread on 18- to 22-mesh canvas. Even when you use the full three-thread strand, separating the threads ("stripping the yarn") before threading the needle will result in fuller stitches and better coverage of the canvas, especially for embroiderers with a tight working tension.

Tapestry yarn (specifically of the type known as Laine Colbert, made by Bon Pasteur or DMC) can be substituted for Persian yarn when you work Basic Stitch or any of its short variations on 10-mesh canvas, or when you work Bargello patterns on 13- or 14-mesh canvas. (Actually I would recommend these tapestry yarns *instead* of Persian yarn for Bargello chair seats or any upholstered pieces that will get some use because tapestry yarns are spun from longer-staple wool and will thus wear better.) These yarns come in an especially wide range of colors, including traditional muted hues, often with up to five gradations each. They are delightful to work with, drawing easily in and out of the canvas, though not separable.

Médicis crewel yarns are very fine single wool threads that can be combined for use on various canvas gauges. Rule of thumb: four strands on 14-mesh canvas, five strands on 13-mesh canvas, and six strands on 12-mesh canvas. For an upholstery piece to be worked in Basic Stitch on 12- to 14-mesh canvas, I would recommend the use of Médicis yarns, again rather than Persian yarns, because of their comparative durability. Their range of colors is limited for the most part, however, to those traditionally used in European crewelwork, so best results are achieved when designs are initially planned around the colors themselves. A tip on Médicis yardage: a 50-gram skein goes about as far as 3 ounces of Persian yarn when you work with four strands on 14-mesh canvas.

Nantucket Twist is a four-ply worsted yarn for needlepoint and crewel. Used as it comes, it covers 12-mesh canvas perfectly and 13- and 14-mesh canvases nearly as well. It can be separated and added to for use on any gauge of canvas. It also has a rather limited range of colors at present, but they are vibrant and inspiring. Spun from long-staple wool, it is long-wearing, less likely to pill and get fuzzy, and is therefore another good choice for a piece that will be upholstered. It is a pleasure to work with as well.

Fawcett linen yarns come in several weights, two of which are used for designs in this book: 10/2 when working in Basic Stitch on 12-mesh canvas, and 10/5 when working on 10-mesh canvas. Also lovely to work with, the linen has a natural sheen that enhances the few, but well-chosen, colors available. A quality of depth is achieved by a slight unevenness in the dyeing. They are not separable.

Six-strand cotton floss is made by a number of manufacturers; the brands are generally interchangeable. Although called six-strand, it is what I refer to as a *strand* consisting of six *threads* that can be separated (as it is used mainly for crewel and counted-thread embroidery), added to, and doubled over, for use in designs in this book. Working in Basic Stitch, use six threads on 14-mesh canvas, eight threads on 12-mesh canvas, and twelve threads on 10-mesh canvas. Rather than use the six-thread strand as it comes, in the first case, separate a yard-long strand into two groups of three threads each. Take one group, thread at one end, and push the needle to the middle; then fold over, all ends together. Leave about an inch at the back of the canvas, and proceed to stitch, working over the ends to anchor them. In this manner, use four threads doubled over when eight threads are required. When twelve threads are required, use a full strand, unseparated, double it over, and anchor the ends. The reason I emphasize anchoring the ends when using cotton floss especially is that this minimizes its tendency to twist, resulting in uneven work. Also, needles like to slip off unanchored ends of cotton floss.

Folklorico's *La Paleta Silk Twist* can be substituted for cotton floss in any of the designs in this book, as can other silk flosses. I recommend using four strands of La Paleta (two doubled over, ends anchored at the back) on 14-mesh canvas, six strands on 12-mesh canvas, and eight strands on 10-mesh canvas.

Other substitutes for cotton floss, with the highest sheen, are *El Molino* for use on 10- and 12-mesh canvases, *Artisan 2-Ply Perlé* on 12-mesh canvas, and *Artisan Globo* on 12- and 14-mesh canvases. They are all rayon flosses from Folklorico. For each, use one full unseparated strand doubled over, anchoring the ends. They are easiest to work with on plain mono canvas.

The sheen of linen, cotton, silk, and synthetic yarns is emphasized by the use of the longer stitches, but even worked in Basic Stitch, these yarns contrast effectively with wool yarns used in the same piece. Outlines requiring cotton floss should be worked first, as should any outlining generally; otherwise, they will be shallow in relation to the surrounding areas worked in wool.

Bucilla Spotlight, available in gold-tone and silver-tone, should be used in single strand on 14-mesh canvas; a small tight knot in the free end will prevent unraveling. *Moonlight*, from Mark Distributors, has the same characteristics as Spotlight and is available in ten metallic colors. *Jacmore Star-Dust Lamé* should be used doubled over, ends anchored at the back, and worked on 12-mesh canvas.

If you want to go as far as using the real thing, Folklorico's *Madrid Collection* features sterling silver and 24-karat gold electroplated threads. Doubled over and anchored, number 29 will cover 14-mesh canvas; number 29++ will cover 12-mesh canvas.

THE STITCHES

Most of the designs in this book are to be worked in what is referred to as Basic Stitch. By this I mean the use of Basketweave or Diagonal Tent Stitch (upper left in Diagram 1), for filling in design areas and background areas, combined with Continental or Horizontal Tent Stitch (lower left in Diagram 1), as well as the other two procedures (in the diagram) for outlining, for veins of leaves, etc. Generally these lines should be worked first, and sometimes you will find it necessary to "pluck," especially when you want to work up or toward the right. With the lines of the design established, filling in with Basketweave Stitch is much easier. You will also find that the greater use of this stitch, wherever possible, will distort your canvas less in the end, whereas complete reliance on Continental Stitch will result in a very trapezoidal canvas that may require two or more blockings.

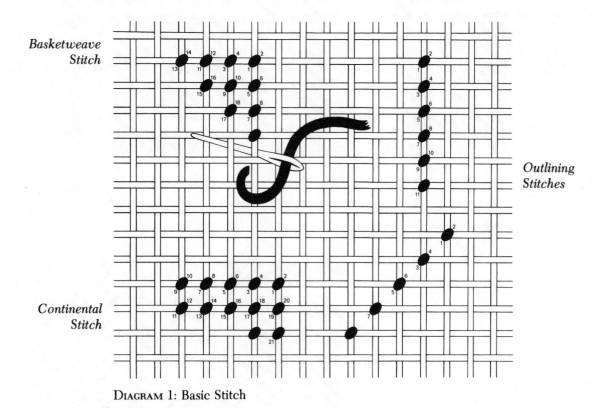

Basketweave Stitch

Outlining Stitches

Continental Stitch

DIAGRAM 1: Basic Stitch

The following diagrams represent combinations of stitches to be used in some of the designs in this book. Note that while any of these stitches may span two or more mesh of canvas, each is really only a variation of the basic slanting stitch covering one mesh. None of the designs requires the use of straight stitches (worked parallel to the canvas mesh, such as upright Gobelin and Bargello stitches).

This is because none of the designs called for the use of straight stitches only, and I decided not to combine slanted and straight stitches in any design. I have found that combining them often results in an inconsistent coverage of the canvas. It is also difficult to express both kinds of stitches in a graph, making the graph very frustrating to follow. One of the reasons some of the designs are graphed on the diagonal within a square piece of canvas is that the effect of the longer stitches worked in rows perpendicular to each other can be achieved in a much more straightforward way. Also, as you've probably discovered, diagonal lines of single-stitch width that cross to form diamonds, etc., don't look alike; the line extending from lower right to upper left will be "stepped." Working these lines as horizontals and verticals within the tilted rectangle solves this problem as well.

Note: Stitch diagrams continue after the color plates.

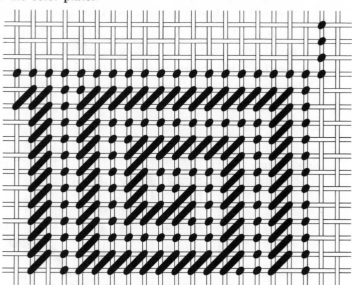

DESIGN 3: Illustrates formation of the meander or fret of Design 22 (Floral Diamonds in Thunderbolt Lattice).

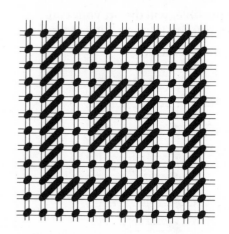

DIAGRAM 2: Illustrates the pattern of stitches used to work the alternate radiating squares of Design 20 (Chrysanthemum Medallion with Cranes).

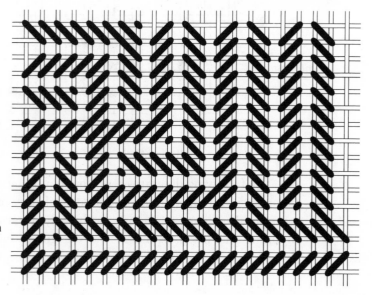

DIAGRAM 4: Represents the construction of the lightning-bolt lattices in designs number 24, 25, and 26.

16

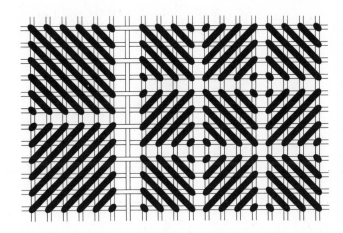

DIAGRAM 5: Illustrates the use of small Scotch stitches to form the bricklike ground pattern of Design 19 (Chrysanthemum Medallions on "Braided Fence").

DIAGRAM 6: Illustrates the use of Scotch stitches as checks, working over 4-by-4-mesh squares (right), as for designs number 17 and 18, and working over 6-by-6-mesh squares (left), as for designs number 5 and 27.

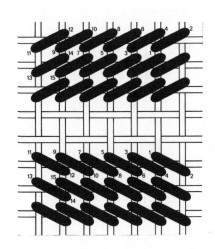

DIAGRAM 7: Represents the Encroaching Gobelin Stitch on an oblique slant to the right (top), used in Design 28 (Chrysanthemums Within a Fence), and to the left (bottom), used in Design 29 ("Flaming Drum").

DIAGRAM 8: Illustrates the combination of Oblique Encroaching Gobelin and Mosaic stitches, outlined with Basic Stitch, as used in Design 21 (Chrysanthemum Medallions with "Nine Stars").

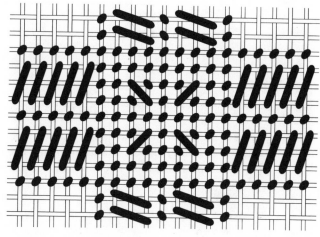

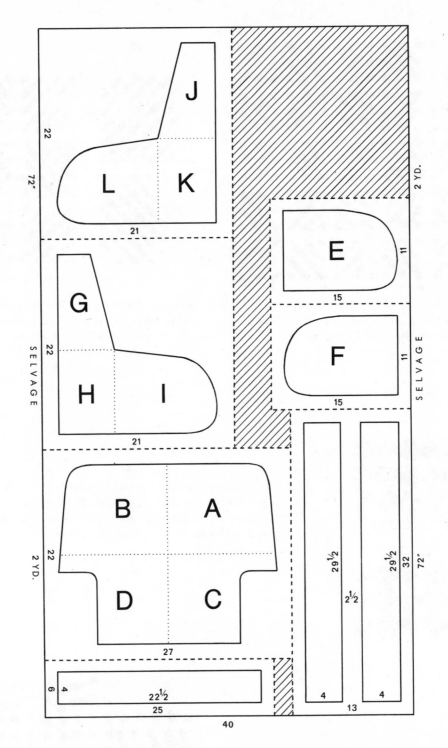

CUTTING DIAGRAM
(See 30. Autumn Grasses with Butterflies, Bed Rest, page 113)
This diagram will help you to visualize the various pieces of the bed rest shown in graphed sections on pages 114 through 121. It also shows the most economical way to cut the canvas pieces needed from just 2 yards of canvas 40 inches wide. (Shaded areas are left over.) The straight arm-rest pieces are to be worked simply in Basic Stitch with the background color (both on one piece of canvas), as is the top strip. Making and finishing the bed rest will require professional skills.

THE DESIGNS

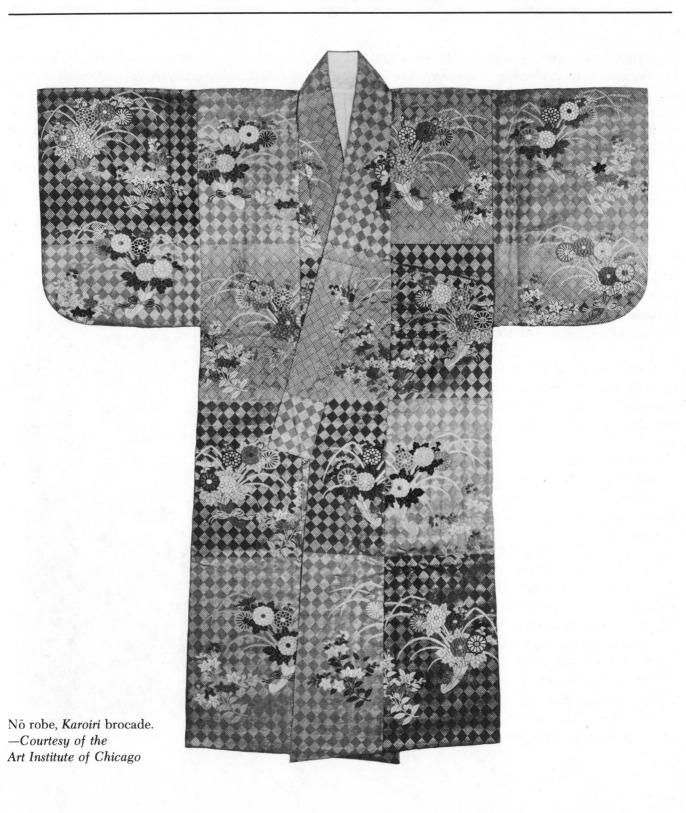

Nō robe, *Karoiri* brocade.
—*Courtesy of the*
Art Institute of Chicago

I. Irises on Basketwork Lattice, Wall Hanging 14″ x 22″

The original eighteenth-century *karaori* robe is said to have been worn for performances of *Kakitsubata* ("The Iris"), a third-category (Woman) Nō, probably by Zeami. In the play, a young village girl recites a poem by Narihira, the poet-aristocrat of the Heian period (794-1185). The poem is an acrostic of *Kakitsubata*, the first syllable of each line forming the five syllables of the word. The girl later reveals herself as the spirit of the iris and dances in gratitude to Narihira for immortalizing the flower.

The basketwork lattice, *kagome*, symbolizes water by its reference to the use of bamboo baskets filled with pebbles to shore up riverbanks and prevent them from crumbling. This associates the pattern with irises because they grow in damp ground, an example of the subtlety of suggestion characteristic of Nō aesthetics.

CANVAS: 12 mesh to the inch. Design covers 169 mesh horizontally by 272 mesh vertically; a piece of canvas at least 18″ by 26″ will be sufficient, allowing 2 inches unworked margin all around for ease in framing.

NEEDLE: #20.

STITCH: Basic Stitch.

YARNS: Nantucket Twist, 2-oz. skeins averaging 147 yd., which when cut yield about 192 strands; use it as it comes:

1) 1 skein #1A "Eggshell"(antique white)
3) 14 strands #49 "Lupin Blue"(light lavender)
5) 1 skein #50 "Wild Violet"

Fawcett 10/2 linen yarn, 15-yd. skeins:

6) 4 skeins "Spanish Gold"
7) 4 skeins "Spring Green"
8) 4 skeins "Chartreuse"
9) 1 skein "Bleached"(white)
10) 2 skeins "Pink"
11) 1 skein "Orange"
12) 1 skein "English Lavender."

NOTE: The color given as #2 on the graph is an intermediate shade achieved by using two threads of color #1 with two threads of color #3. Similarly, use two threads of color #3 with two threads of color #5 to achieve intermediate shade #4. (The four-thread strand of Nantucket Twist should be separated at the middle of each strand, two pairs of two threads each being gently pulled apart.)

2. Peonies with Butterflies, Lady's Rocker

CANVAS: 10 mesh to the inch, preferably plain mono or tan penelope. The floral design spans 13½″ by 22½″ for the rocker back, 15″ by 17″ for the seat. To cover a similar rocker or chair of any size, center the design, and continue the lattice pattern out, following the shape of a carefully taken template. (As always for upholstery pieces, allow *at least* 2 inches of unworked margin all around, not only for ease in upholstering, but also in case you need to add more worked area.)

NEEDLE: #18

STITCH: Basic Stitch.

YARNS: (Amounts given were required to work a piece 20″ by 29″ for the back and a piece 27″ by 25″ for the seat; adjust floss and background-yarn amounts to cover a larger or smaller chair.)

DMC cotton floss, Article #117, 8-meter skeins (8.7 yd.); use full six-thread strand doubled over to make twelve threads, ends anchored (see YARNS):

1) 40 skeins #783 (bright antique gold)

Bon Pasteur Laine Colbert tapestry yarn, 11-yd. skeins; use one full strand:

2) 80 skeins #143 (light mist blue)
3) 4 skeins #330 (ecru)
4) 8 skeins #33 (light maize yellow)
5) 6 skeins #683 (coral)
6) 6 skeins #934 (jade)
7) 7 skeins #795 (juniper).

NOTE: Work gold floral outlines and background lattice with the floss *first*, so that they do not recede below the level of areas worked with wool yarn. Also, cross-stitch the dots in the butterflies' wings to make them more prominent.

3. Fans and Scrolls, Chair Seat

This design was adapted from an Edo period (1603-1868, also known as the Tokugawa period) costume of the type known as *nuihaku*, denoting the use of elaborate embroidery on gold- or silver-foil-painted ground fabrics.

CANVAS: 14 mesh to the inch. Design covers 306 mesh horizontally by 288 mesh vertically; a piece of canvas at least 24″ by 22½″ will be sufficient. It is planned for a surface area about 19″ at its widest point by 15″ deep, plus extra area for drop and turn-under.

NEEDLE: #22.

STITCH: Basic Stitch.

YARNS: Médicis crewel yarn, 50-gram skeins; use four strands held together:

1) 28 grams #502 bis (antique white)
2) 6 grams #411 (medium-light fern green)
3) 6 grams #407 (medium jade green)
4) 6 grams #104 (rust)
5) 18 grams #506 (dark steel blue)
6) 6 grams #128 (coral)
7) 3 grams #122 (dusty mauve)
8) 102 grams (2 skeins plus 2 grams) #322 (golden camel).

4. Ivy Scrolls, Footstool Top 20″ x 16″ OVAL

This design comes from a *maiginu* ("dancing silk") jacket, reserved for the protagonist of a third-category (Woman) Nō play, a maiden who performs a dream-like dance, *jonomai*. The lushness of ivy covering the entire surface is intended to suggest this quality of femininity, while the gold-brocaded (*kinran*) silk of the original costume conveys the mood of splendor and solemnity characteristic of Nō plays.

CANVAS: 14 mesh to the inch. Oval design covers 286 mesh horizontally by 230 mesh vertically at its widest points; a piece of canvas 24″ by 20″ will be sufficient. This worked area will cover a footstool top with 16″ by 12″ surface dimensions, such as the one pictured, manufactured by Empire Wood Carving Company (see SOURCES), allowing an extra 4 inches in each direction for drop and turn-under.

NEEDLE: #22.

STITCH: Basic Stitch.

YARNS: DMC cotton floss, Article #117, 8-meter skeins (8.7 yd.); use six threads (see YARNS):

1) 15 skeins #729 (antique gold)

Médicis crewel yarn, 50-gram skeins; use four strands held together:

2) 67 grams #106 (claret)
3) 4 grams #103 bis (light pink)
4) 4 grams #407 (medium jade green)
5) 6 grams #210 (light blue)
6) 4 grams #128 (coral)
7) 4 grams #411 (medium-light fern green)
8) 5 grams #409 (deep blue green)
9) 2 grams #502 bis (antique white).

5. Clematis Scrolls on Checked Ground, Cushion APPROXIMATELY 17″ x 13″

The name of the type of costume from which this design is adapted, *atsuita karaori*, refers to its having been woven of silk floss with long floats across the surface of the fabric resembling embroidery (*karaori*) and to its being used for male roles (*atsuita*), probably as an inner robe. The light blue in its ground pattern of *ishidatami* checks is meant to balance any effect of heaviness resulting from such a lavish use of golds.

CANVAS: 14 mesh to the inch. Design covers 240 mesh horizontally by 180 mesh vertically; a piece of canvas 19″ by 15″ will be sufficient.

NEEDLE: #22.

STITCH: Basic Stitch for scroll design, to be worked first; then Scotch Stitch variation covering six canvas mesh, in two colors. See STITCHES, Diagram 6, page 17.

YARNS: DMC cotton floss, Article #117, 8-meter skeins (8.7 yd.); use six threads (see YARNS):

1) 2 skeins #992 (medium blue-green)
2) 2 skeins #605 (light hot pink)
3) 3 skeins #552 (medium lilac)
4) 6 skeins #783 (bright antique gold)
5) 10 skeins #744 (light maize)
6) 7 skeins #3325 (light blue)
7) 3 skeins #352 (melon)

NOTE: First work the leaf and outline areas of the scroll design, then work the inner colors of the floral motifs, and finally, work the ground pattern. You will notice that the left half of the design repeats the right half formally; only the inner colors of the floral motifs are varied. Therefore, you may find this basic design versatile for other objects with large surface areas, such as chairs, benches, etc., as you can repeat it *ad infinitum*, varying only its inner colors to achieve fresh, unexpected effects. The design would also be useful for a rug to be worked in the manner of Design 19.

6. Cherry Blossoms on Diamond Lattice, Tea Cozy 14½″ x 11½″

From naturalistic clematis blossoms in the preceding design, we move on to the more stylized cherry blossoms of this one, yet with a softer ground pattern.

CANVAS: 14 mesh to the inch. Design covers 205 mesh horizontally by 162 mesh vertically at its widest points; a piece of canvas 16½″ by 13½″ will be sufficient.

NEEDLE: #20.

STITCH: Basic Stitch.

YARNS: DMC cotton floss, Article #117, 8-meter skeins (8.7 yd.); use six threads (see YARNS):

1) 2 skeins "Snow-White" (true white)

2) 2 skeins #605 (light hot pink)

3) 3 skeins #352 (melon)

Bucilla Spotlight gold-tone metallic yarn, 20-gram skeins (.7 oz., or about 130 yd.); use single strand:

4) ⅓ skein

Persian yarn; separate the strand to use two threads:

5) 2 oz. (about 80 yd.) medium olive green (such as Bucilla #28, Paternayan #553, Spinnerin #4185, or Paragon #645).

NOTE: Work lattice and outlines in the metallic yarn first.

7. Plum Blossoms on Pine-Bark Lattice, Bellpull 4" x 36"

The pine-bark lozenge (*matsukawa-bishi*) belongs to the group of diamond motifs called *hishigata*. While the shape does not actually represent pine bark, calling it by this name seems to give it poetic overtones; conversely, simplifying a natural form to a symmetrical lozenge motif is thought to impart a feeling of *iki* (connoting chic, by the use of "pure" form, as opposed to *yabo*, considered trite).

CANVAS: 10 mesh to the inch. Design covers 41 mesh horizontally by 363 mesh vertically. A piece of canvas 6" by 40" will be sufficient, allowing extra canvas at the ends for ease in mounting.

NEEDLE: #18.

STITCH: Basic Stitch.

YARNS: Fawcett 10/5 linen yarn, 15-yd. skeins:

1) 7 skeins "Gold"

Persian yarn, unseparated:

2) 20 yd. (about ½ oz.) medium turquoise (such as DMC "Floralia" #7608)

3) 40 yd. (about 1 oz.) medium coral (such as DMC "Floralia" #7106)

4) 20 yd. deep china blue (such as DMC "Floralia" #7296)

NOTE: The piece was mounted with Jacmore's bell-pull hardware #2553/4".

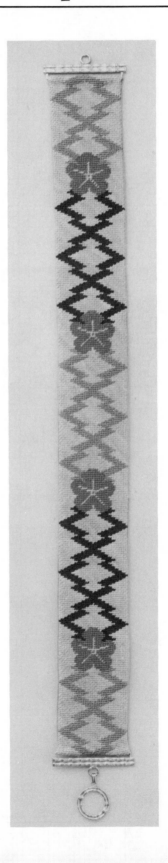

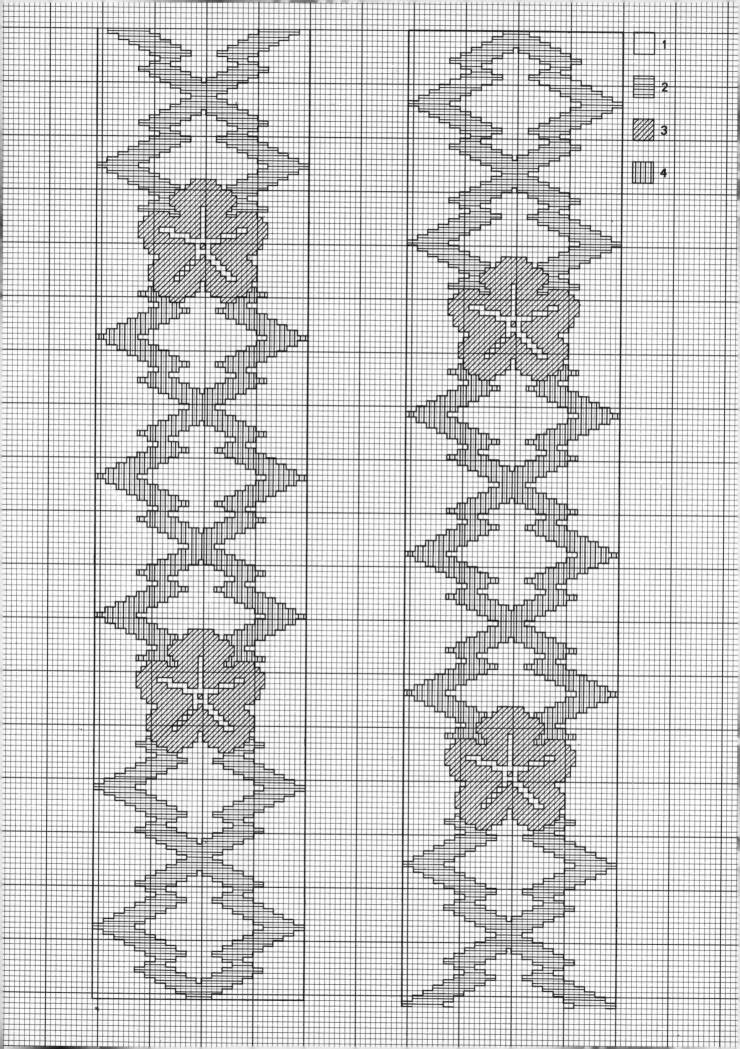

8. Peony on Pine-Bark Lattice, Cushion 16″ x 13″ OVAL

Pine-bark lozenges are repeated to form the lattice ground of this design, which, in metallic gold, adds richness, weight, and angularity to contrast with the more natural coloring and asymmetry of the peonies.

CANVAS: 10 mesh to the inch. Oval design covers 163 mesh horizontally by 133 mesh vertically at its widest points; a piece of canvas 18½″ by 15½″ will be sufficient.

NEEDLE: #18.

STITCH: Basic Stitch.

YARNS: Bucilla Spotlight gold-tone metallic yarn, 20-gram skeins (.7 oz., or about 130 yd.); use two strands (one doubled over, ends anchored):

1) 1 skein

Bon Pasteur Laine Colbert tapestry yarn, 11-yd. skeins; use one full strand:

2) 2 skeins #35 (rich gold)
3) 3 skeins #683 (coral)
4) 1 skein #645 (henna)
5) 2 skeins #143 (light china blue)
6) 2 skeins #116 (deep china blue)
7) 2 skeins #803 (light moss green)
8) 2 skeins #936 (jade).

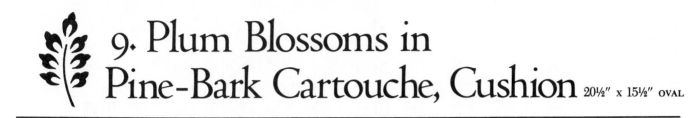

9. Plum Blossoms in Pine-Bark Cartouche, Cushion 20½″ x 15½″ OVAL

Here the pine-bark motif becomes a cartouche enclosing naturalistic plum blossoms in an implied space contrasted with the *karahana* (Chinese flower) lattice, abstract and very much on the surface. This and the previous design illustrate well the subtle juxtaposition of opposites—geometric and pictorial motifs, regularity and asymmetry, monochrome and color—which caused the brocades woven in the Nishijin district of Kyoto to be in great demand for Nō costumes from the sixteenth century on.

CANVAS: 10 mesh to the inch. Oval design covers 205 mesh horizontally by 155 mesh vertically at its widest points; a piece of canvas 23″ by 18″ will be sufficient.

NEEDLE: #18.

STITCH: Basic Stitch.

YARNS: Bucilla Spotlight gold-tone metallic yarn, 20-gram skeins (.7 oz., or about 130 yd.); use two strands (one doubled over, ends anchored):

1) 1 skein

Bon Pasteur Laine Colbert tapestry yarn, 11-yd. skeins; use one full strand:

2) 14 skeins #674 (antique gold)
3) 1 skein #191 (antique white)
4) 1 skein #12 (coral)
5) 1 skein #242 (deep rose)
6) 1 skein #685 (terra-cotta)
7) 7 skeins #423 (ash blond).

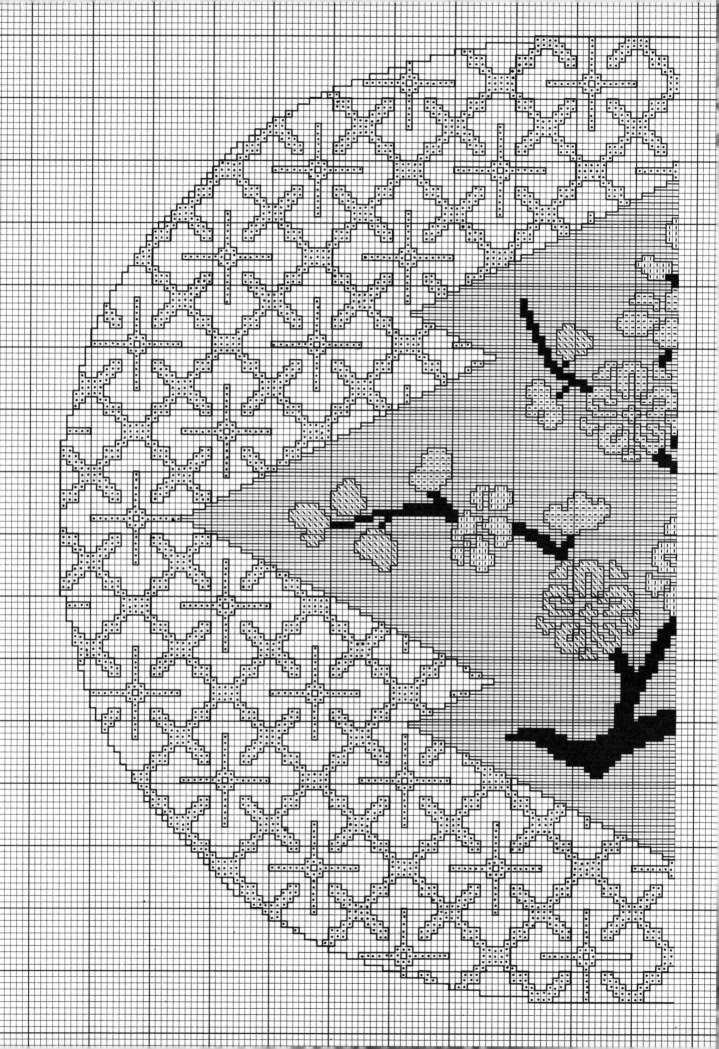

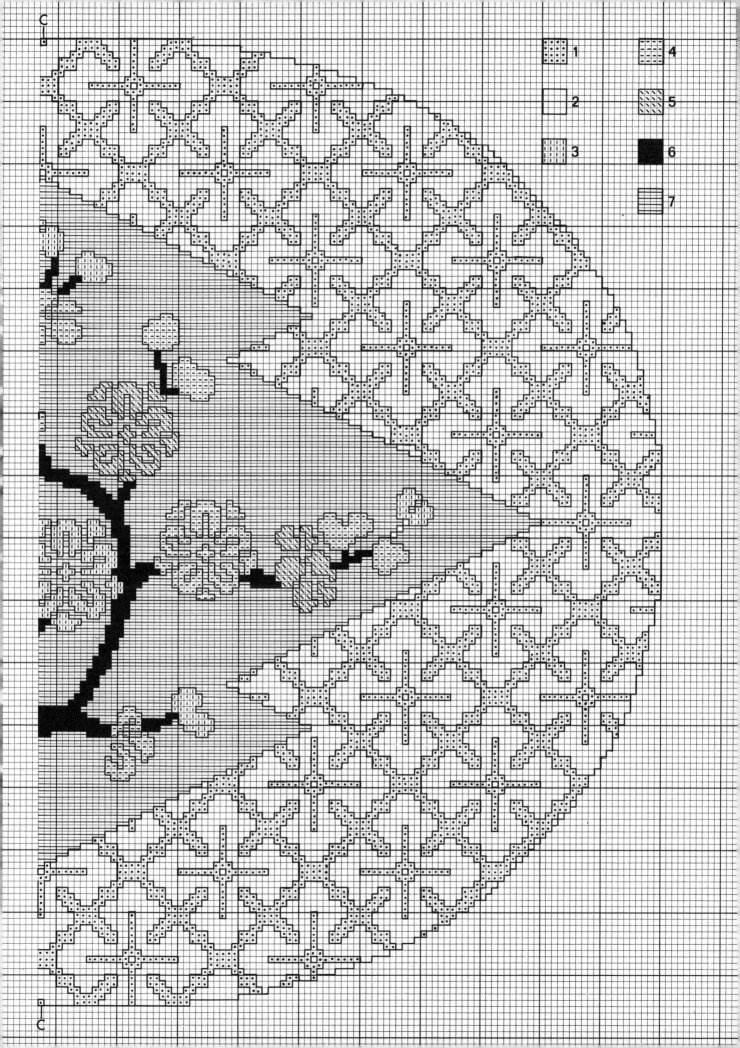

10. Cloud Gong on Tortoiseshell Lattice, Mirror 15" x 27½"

The eighteenth-century *atsuita karaori* robe from which this design was adapted featured large *umban* (derived from the cloud-shaped bronze gong used in Zen monasteries to announce mealtimes and meditation periods) floating on a lattice ground pattern of tortoiseshell hexagons, *kikkō*.

CANVAS: 14 mesh to the inch. Design covers 215 mesh horizontally by 389 mesh vertically; a piece of canvas 19" by 31½" will be sufficient, allowing 2 inches unworked margin for ease in framing. (Leave unworked area for mirror intact until piece is finished and framed; the same style of gilt strip should be used to outline the mirror as is used for the outer frame.)

NEEDLE: #20.

STITCH: Basic Stitch.

YARNS: Bucilla Spotlight gold-tone metallic yarn, 20-gram skeins (.7 oz., or about 130 yd.); use single strand:

1) 1 skein

Persian yarn; separate the strand to use two threads:

2) 40 yd. ivory

3) 70 yd. light blue (such as Bucilla #42, Paternayan #B43, Columbia-Minerva #B42, or Paragon #172)

4) 50 yd. medium violet (such as Bucilla #71, Paternayan #650, Columbia-Minerva #650, or Paragon #427)

5) 50 yd. juniper (such as Bucilla #47, Paternayan #530, Columbia-Minerva #530, or Paragon #231)

6) 50 yd. coral (such as Bucilla #34, Paternayan #R86, Columbia-Minerva #R70, or Paragon #225)

7) 50 yd. brick rose (such as Bucilla #61, Paternayan #211, Columbia-Minerva #211, or Paragon #389).

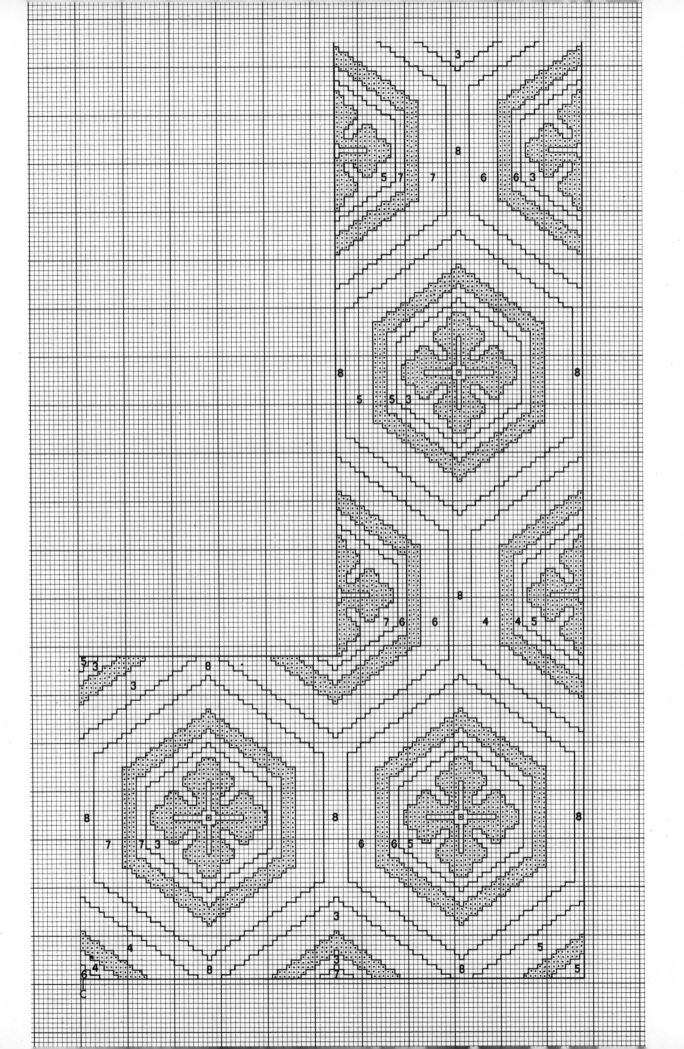

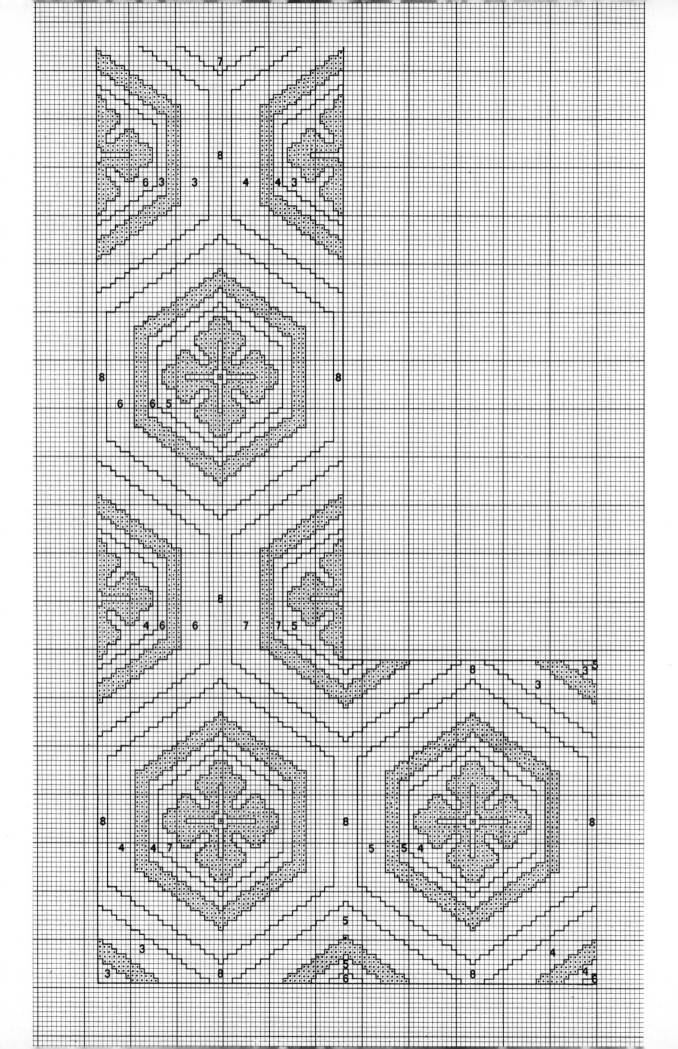

II. Cloud Gong on Tortoiseshell Lattice, Director's Chair

The graph, directions, and yarn amounts given are for making a back and seat cover for a standard-size director's chair, although the chair pictured is a smaller version of the style. Working the graph as given will yield a back piece 29½″ by 6½″ and a seat piece 22″ by 15″. The pieces should be attached to the canvas back and seat that come with your chair, rather than used alone; the space between the ends of the back piece should be lined with compatible-color fabric with good body. A nice finishing touch is to work a binding stitch along the long edges of the piece before mounting.

CANVAS: 14 mesh to the inch. Back design covers 415 mesh horizontally by 93 mesh vertically; a piece of canvas 33½″ by 10½″ will be sufficient, allowing 2 inches unworked margin all around. Seat design covers 307 mesh horizontally by 209 mesh vertically; a piece of canvas 26″ by 19″ will be sufficient, allowing 2 extra inches all around as well.

NEEDLE: #22.

STITCH: Basic Stitch.

YARNS: Médicis crewel yarn, 50-gram* skeins; use four strands held together:
1) 13 grams #502 bis (antique white)
2) 11 grams #304 bis (light gold)
3) 23 grams #128 (coral)
4) 15 grams #324 (greenish gold)
5) 26 grams #203 (grayish blue)
6) 65 grams #411 (medium-light fern green)
7) 35 grams #106 (claret)
8) 27 grams #124 bis (deep plum)
9) 35 grams #104 (rust)

DMC cotton floss, Article #117, 8-meter skeins (8.7 yd.); use six threads (see YARNS):
10) 26 skeins #783 (bright antique gold).

NOTE: It's best to work dotted areas given in graph using color #10 (bright antique gold) first. Inner-flower "crosses" are to be worked using the same color of yarn as surrounds each flower.

12. Tortoiseshell Lattice, Bellpull 7″ x 35″

The piece was mounted with Jacmore's bellpull hardware style #2561/7″ (see SOURCES) and backed with gold velveteen.

CANVAS: 10 mesh to the inch. Design covers 70 mesh horizontally by 356 mesh vertically; a piece of canvas 9″ by 40″ will be sufficient, allowing 2 inches unworked margin at top and bottom for ease in mounting.

NEEDLE: #18.

STITCH: Basic Stitch.

YARNS: DMC cotton floss, Article #117, 8-meter skeins (8.7 yd.); use full six-thread strand doubled over to make twelve threads, ends anchored (see YARNS):

1) 24 skeins #783 (bright antique gold)

Bon Pasteur Laine Colbert tapestry yarn, 11-yd. skeins; use one full strand:

2) 4 skeins #330 (ecru)
3) 4 skeins #143 (light mist blue)
4) 3 skeins #116 (deep china blue)
5) 4 skeins #803 (light moss green)
6) 4 skeins #936 (jade)
7) 7 skeins #225 (medium rosy rust)
8) 4 skeins #521 (lilac)
9) 4 skeins #625 (magenta).

13. Joined-Circle Lattice, Bellpull 5″ x 33″

An embroidered headband, *kazura-obi*, inspired this design of *shippo-tsunagi*, joined circles, a classical *yū-soku* motif of Chinese origin, enriched with *karahana*, Chinese flowers. This lattice motif with its origins in Buddhist art of the Heian period (794-1185) was especially favored for Nō costumes because the meaning of the word *shippo* (seven treasures or jewels) was considered auspicious.

CANVAS: 14 mesh to the inch. Design covers 74 mesh horizontally by 474 mesh vertically; a strip of canvas 7″ by 35″ (or 37″ if extra turn-under is required for finishing) will be sufficient.

NEEDLE: #20.

STITCH: Basic Stitch.

YARNS: Bucilla Spotlight gold-tone metallic yarn, 20-gram skeins (.7 oz., or about 130 yd.); use single strand:

1) about ⅔ skein

Persian yarn; separate the strand to use two threads:

2) 26 yd. wine red (such as Bucilla #145, Paternayan #236, Spinnerin #4328, or Columbia-Minerva #236)

3) 22 yd. light blue (such as Bucilla #173, Paternayan #781, Spinnerin #4440, or Columbia-Minerva #395)

4) 4 oz. antique gold (such as Bucilla #20, Paternayan #445, Spinnerin #4646, or Columbia-Minerva #445).

NOTE: Bellpull is finished with Jacmore's hardware style #2561/5″.

14. Maple Leaves on Joined-Circle Lattice, Cushion 18″ x 18″

Here the tranquil regularity of the *shippo-tsunagi* lattice used as a ground pattern (*jimon*) becomes a foil for the surface pattern (*uwamon*) of large, dynamic maple leaves.

CANVAS: 14 mesh to the inch. Design covers a 249-mesh square; a square of canvas 20″ by 20″ will be sufficient.

NEEDLE: #22.

STITCH: Basic Stitch.

YARNS: DMC cotton floss, Article #117, 8-meter skeins (8.7 yd.); use six threads (see YARNS):

1) 7 skeins #783 (bright antique gold)
2) 6 skeins #744 (light maize)
3) 3 skeins Ecru
4) 5 skeins #352 (melon)
5) 11 skeins #991 (dark blue green)

Persian yarn; separate the strand to use two threads:

6) 4 oz. terra-cotta (such as Paternayan #225, Bucilla #5, Spinnerin #4625, or DMC "Floralia" #7125).

C

15. Maple Leaves and Butterfly, Cushion 17″ x 14″

This and the following design are adapted from a seventeenth-century costume of silk embroidery on gold-painted satin ground, *nuihaku*.

CANVAS: 12 mesh to the inch. Design covers 202 mesh horizontally by 170 mesh vertically; a piece of canvas at least 19″ by 16″ will be sufficient.

NEEDLE: #22.

STITCH: Basic Stitch.

YARNS: Fawcett 10/2 linen yarn, 15 yd. skeins:

1) 17 skeins "Gold"

Nantucket Twist, 2-oz. skeins averaging 147 yd., which when cut yield about 192 strands; use it as it comes:

2) 20 strands #1A Eggshell (antique white)

3) 20 strands #15A Topaz (bright medium gold)

4) 10 strands #28 Cranberry Pink (bright coral)

5) 24 strands #63 Turquoise

6) 2 strands #47 Pansy (violet)

7) 37 strands #11 Old Bronze (medium-light olive green)

8) 20 strands #108 Juniper (dark blue-green).

30.

23.

12.

10.

11.

1.

5.   6.

27.   4.   2.

7.   13.

3.

29.

17.   18.

19.

16. 15.

22.

20.

14. **21.**

25. **26.**

16. Chrysanthemums and Butterfly, Cushion 17″ x 14″

CANVAS: 12 mesh to the inch. Design covers 202 mesh horizontally by 170 mesh vertically; a piece of canvas at least 19″ by 16″ will be sufficient.

NEEDLE: #22.

STITCH: Basic Stitch.

YARNS: Fawcett 10/2 linen yarn, 15-yd. skeins:

1) 17 skeins "Gold"

Nantucket Twist, 2-oz. skeins averaging 147 yd., which when cut yield about 192 strands; use it as it comes:

2) 15 strands #1A Eggshell (antique white)
3) 16 strands #15A Topaz (bright medium gold)
4) 14 strands #28 Cranberry Pink (bright coral)
5) 22 strands #63 Turquoise
6) 18 strands #47 Pansy (violet)
7) 30 strands #11 Old Bronze (medium-light olive green)
8) 18 strands #108 Juniper (dark blue-green).

17. Chrysanthemum Medallions on Checked Ground, Ivory Evening Bag

Conventionalized chrysanthemums of the previous designs are here isolated on a subtle geometric ground pattern of *ishidatami* checks.

CANVAS: 12 mesh to the inch. Design covers 108 mesh horizontally by 144 mesh vertically; a piece of canvas 11″ by 14″ will be sufficient.

NEEDLE: #20.

STITCHES: Basic Stitch for chrysanthemum motifs; to work ground pattern, see STITCHES, Diagram 6, right, page 17.

YARNS: DMC cotton floss, Article #117, 8-meter skeins (8.7 yd.); use eight threads (see YARNS):

1) 3 skeins #783 (bright antique gold)
2) 6 skeins Ecru

Nantucket Twist, 2-oz. skeins averaging 147 yd., which when cut yield about 192 strands; use it as it comes:

3) ½ skein #1A Eggshell
4) 17 strands #28 Cranberry Pink (hot coral)
5) 36 strands #50 Wild Violet
6) 17 strands #69 Wave Blue (medium turquoise).

NOTE: This 6″ by 5″ bag was finished with Jacmore's gold frame #1063/6″ (see SOURCES). Request "Stitch-A-Bag" instructions with this hardware for finishing.

68

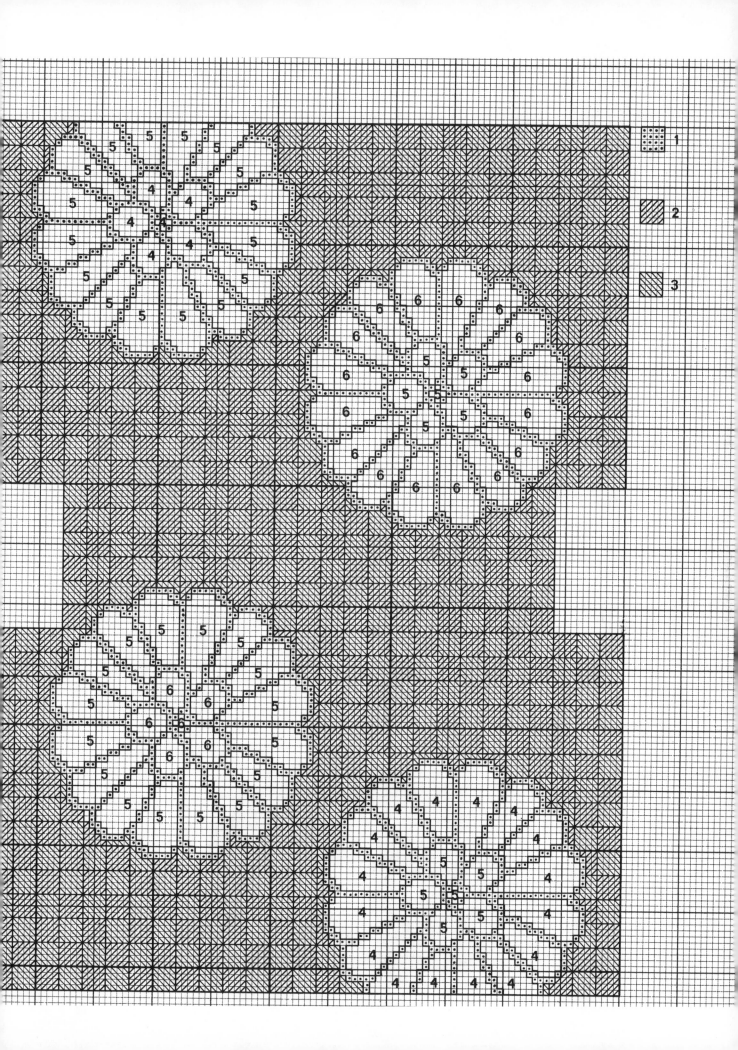

18. Chrysanthemum Medallions on Checked Ground, Blue Evening Bag

Larger, more dimensional chrysanthemum medallions on a darker ground of *ishidatami* checks impart more of a feeling of dignity to a design basically the same as Design 17.

CANVAS: 12 mesh to the inch. Design covers 108 mesh horizontally by 144 mesh vertically; a piece of canvas 11″ by 14″ will be sufficient.

NEEDLE: #20.

STITCHES: Basic Stitch for chrysanthemum motifs; to work ground pattern, see STITCHES, Diagram 6, right, page 17.

YARNS: Jacmore Star-Dust Lamé, Article #255/3, gold, 75-yd. skeins; use two strands (one doubled over, see YARNS, page 13):

1) 1 skein

DMC cotton floss, Article #117, 8-meter skeins (8.7 yd.); use eight threads (see YARNS, page 13):

2) 10 skeins #517 (dark teal blue)

Persian yarn; separate the strand to use two threads:

3) 2 oz. dark teal blue to match #2 above (such as Paternayan #750, Columbia-Minerva #773, Spinnerin #4488, or DMC "Floralia" #7995)

4) 20 yd. coral (such as Paternayan #R60, Columbia-Minerva #R60, Spinnerin #4224, or DMC Floralia #7892)

5) 20 yd. ivory.

NOTE: This 6″ by 5″ bag was finished with Jacmore's gold frame #1063/6″ (see SOURCES). Request "Stitch-A-Bag" instructions with this hardware for finishing.

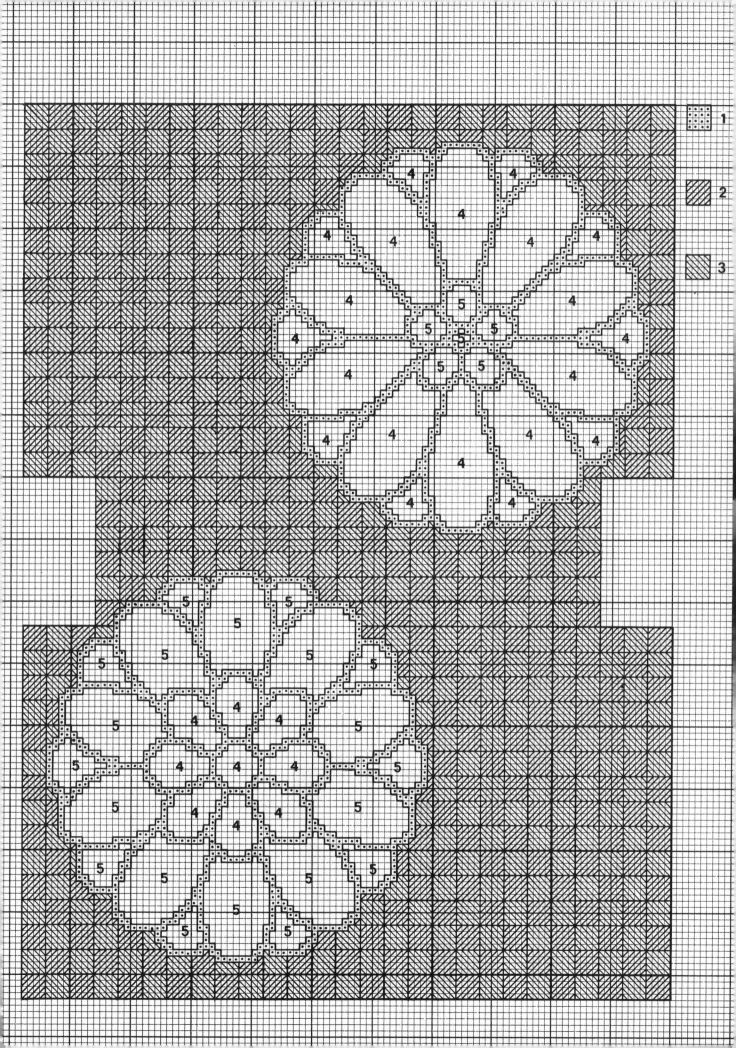

19. Chrysanthemum Medallions on "Braided Fence," Rug 23" x 34"

Large chrysanthemum medallions of many colors, sometimes overlapping, float on a lattice ground pattern representing a stylized braided cypress fence, *higaki*. The finished piece was edged with a binding stitch and backed with wool.

CANVAS: 14 mesh to the inch. Design covers 324 mesh horizontally by 480 mesh vertically; a piece of canvas 27" by 38" will be sufficient, allowing 2 inches unworked margin all around for ease in finishing.

NEEDLE: #22.

STITCHES: Basic Stitch for chrysanthemum medallions; for ground pattern, see STITCHES, Diagram 5, page 17.

YARNS: DMC cotton floss, Article #117, 8-meter skeins (8.7 yd.); use six threads (see YARNS):

1) 45 skeins #783 (bright antique gold)

Médicis crewel yarn, 50-gram skeins; use four strands held together:

2) 4 skeins #106 (claret)
3) 25 grams #407 (medium jade green)
4) 25 grams #208 (medium blue)
5) 25 grams #206 (dark blue)
6) 25 grams #128 (coral)
7) 23 grams #502 bis (antique white)
8) 25 grams #304 bis (light gold).

NOTE: Background areas between the bricklike shapes are also to be worked with yarn color #1 (bright antique gold floss). The bricks are to be worked with color #2 (claret Médicis).

20. Chrysanthemum Medallion with Cranes, Cushion 15½" x 15½"

In this design from an Edo period *atsuita karaori* robe, a large abstract chrysanthemum is centered on a ground pattern of alternating concentric squares and lozenges of paired cranes, *tsuru-bishi*. The Japanese crane is both a symbol of love since it mates for life and a symbol of longevity as in folklore it lives for a thousand years, thereby reinforcing the motif, originally Chinese, of paired birds to signify marital fidelity.

CANVAS: 14 mesh to the inch. Design covers a 215-mesh square; a square of canvas at least 17½" by 17½" will be sufficient.

NEEDLE: #22.

STITCHES: Basic Stitch for chrysanthemum and crane lozenges; to work concentric squares, see STITCHES, Diagram 2, page 16.

YARNS: Persian yarn; separate the strand to use two threads:

1) 25 yd. bright gold (such as Bucilla #3, Paternayan #440, Paragon #206, or Brunswick #8)

2) 40 yd. dark turquoise (such as Bucilla #24, Paternayan #750, Paragon #360, or Brunswick #58)

3) 25 yd. light blue (such as Bucilla #137, Paternayan #758, Paragon #252, or Brunswick #97)

4) 25 yd. terra-cotta (such as Bucilla #5, Paternayan #225, Paragon #483, or Brunswick #72)

5) 40 yd. bright red (such as Bucilla #35, Paternayan #R50, Paragon #224, or Brunswick #209)

6) 18 yd. lime green (such as Bucilla #74, Paternayan #574, Paragon #713, or Brunswick #26)

7) 125 yd. ivory.

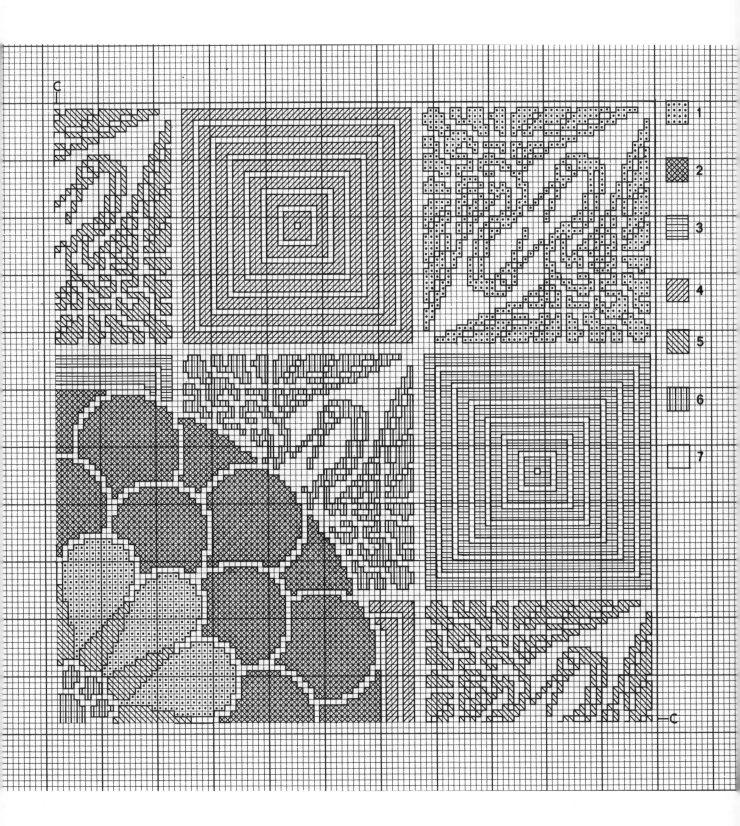

80

81

21. Chrysanthemum Medallions with "Nine Stars," Cushion 16¼" x 9¾"

The chrysanthemum motif of the previous design is here cropped at opposite corners of an asymmetrical rectangular composition. The "nine stars" flowerlike motif derives from Indian astrology to represent the nine planets with Saturn at its center. As an element of esoteric Buddhism it entered Japan representing, it is said, the mandala of Buddhist guardians centering on Dainichi and came to be used as a family crest, *mon*.

CANVAS: 13 mesh to the inch. Design is set on the diagonal within a square 241 mesh by 241 mesh, about 18½" by 18½". Center the design within a square of canvas 23" by 23", allowing more than 2 inches from each point of the design to canvas edge so that the finished piece can be cut out an inch from work all around before its edges are rebound for blocking. Block as a rectangle.

NEEDLE: #20.

STITCHES: Basic Stitch for chrysanthemums and "nine stars" motifs; to work lattices, see STITCHES, Diagram 8, page 17. Work the unmarked rows outlining the lattice areas on the graph in "Snow-White". Use full strand of cotton floss doubled over to make twelve threads when working oblique Gobelin Stitch.

YARNS: Persian yarn; separate the strand to use two threads:

1) 60 yd. terra-cotta (such as Bucilla #5, Paternayan #225, Paragon #483, or Brunswick #72)
DMC cotton floss, Article #117, 8-meter skeins (8.7 yd.); use six threads, except as noted above:
2) 9 skeins #783 (bright antique gold)
3) 3 skeins "Snow-White"
4) 1 skein #3325 (light blue)
5) 2 skeins #517 (dark teal blue)
6) 1 skein #913 (medium-light jade green)
7) 3 skeins #352 (melon)
8) 3 skeins #744 (light maize).

NOTE: The best way to approach this design will be from the lower-right-hand corner rather than from the upper-right, as is usual. An inch diagonally from the lower-right point of your piece of canvas, and just within your marked-off 241-mesh square, start counting mesh diagonally toward the center, as indicated in the graph. The forty-ninth mesh will be within the "nine stars" motif to be worked in color #7 (melon floss). Work this motif, then its background in color #1 (terra-cotta Persian yarn), continuing into the adjacent chrysanthemum motif to outline it. This done, work the vertical and horizontal one-stitch-wide bars in "Snow-White" floss, forming the structure of the design. Check your count frequently. You will then only have to fill in the areas thus defined.

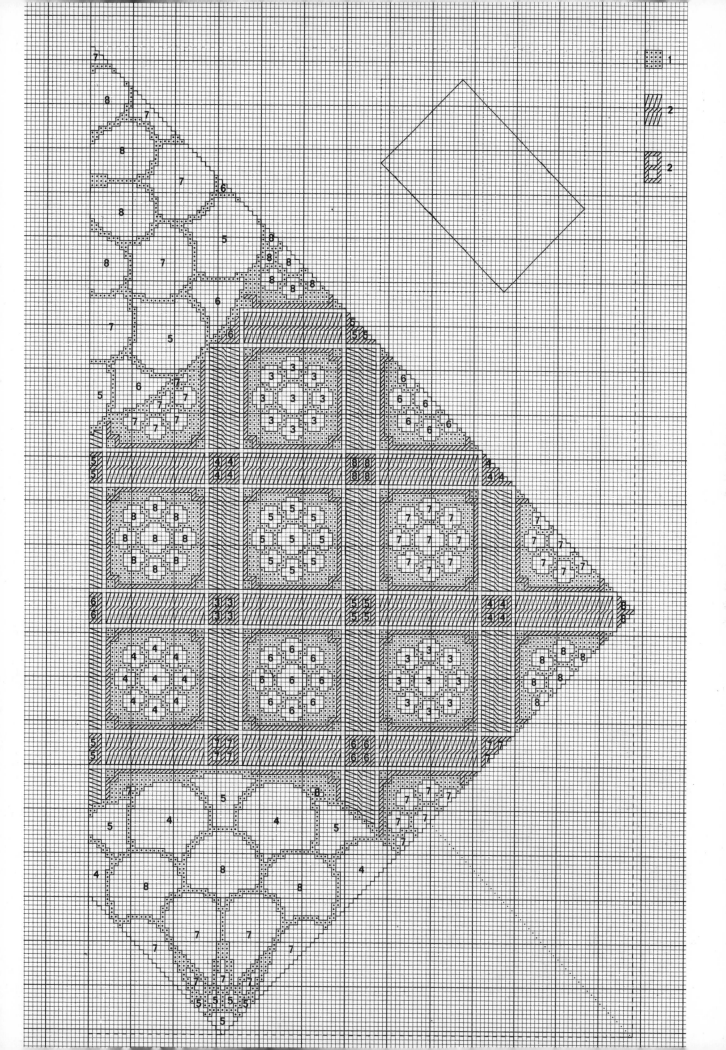

22. Floral Diamonds in Thunderbolt Lattice, Cushion 18" x 15"

Classical *yūsoku* motifs (of Chinese origin) form the ground pattern (*jimon*) of this design, of which the original thunderbolt (*kaminari*) key-fret motif was woven in the *karaori* floating weft popular in the Momoyama period (1568-1603). Enclosed in the borders are sets of four-petaled *karahana*, Chinese flowers.

CANVAS: 14 mesh to the inch, interlocked. Design is set on the diagonal within a square 343 mesh by 343 mesh, about 24½" by 24½". Center the design within a square of canvas 29" by 29", allowing more than 2 inches from each point of the design to the canvas edge, so that the finished piece can be cut out an inch from the work all around before its edges are rebound for blocking. The originally square design will have become a rectangle, and the floral diamonds will have been elongated to lozenge shapes. Block to straighten the sides, as usual, and to remove surface ripples; this may require two blockings (see BLOCKING).

NEEDLE: #22.

STITCHES: Basic Stitch for floral motifs and outlining; to work fret motifs, see STITCHES, Diagram 3, page 16.

YARNS: Persian yarn; separate the strand to use two threads:

1) 20 yd. light antique gold (such as Brunswick #184)

2) 30 yd. sky blue (such as Brunswick #97)

3) 25 yd. medium blue green (such as Brunswick #250)

4) 70 yd. antique white (such as Brunswick #45)

5) 100 yd. coral (such as Brunswick #119)

6) 20 yd. burgundy (such as Brunswick #81).

NOTE: Work the single stitch within the "X" of the middle of each flower with the same color of yarn indicated for its petals on the graph.

23. Swallows and Willow Branches, Miniature Screen 8″ x 10½″ OPENINGS

Besides the motif of swallows and willows, the repertory of bird and flower motifs includes such combinations as bush warbler and plum blossom, phoenix and paulownia, herons and rushes, and sparrows and bamboo. The custom miniature screen was made by Norman Jernigan (see SOURCES).

CANVAS: 14 mesh to the inch. Each panel design is set on the diagonal within a square 191 mesh by 191 mesh; a square of canvas 16″ by 16″ will be sufficient, allowing more than an inch unworked margin all around.

NEEDLE: #20.

STITCHES: Basic Stitch for everything but the lightning-bolt motif (*saya-gata*), which should be worked according to Diagram 4 (see STITCHES, page 16.)

YARNS: DMC cotton floss, Article #117, 8-meter skeins (8.7 yd.); use six threads (see YARNS):

1) 6 skeins #809 (light blue)

Bucilla Spotlight gold-tone metallic yarn, 20-gram skeins (.7 oz., or about 130 yd.); use single strand:

2) about ½ skein

Médicis crewel yarn, 50-gram skeins; use four strands held together:

3) 10 grams #502 bis (antique white)

4) 2½ skeins #208 (medium blue).

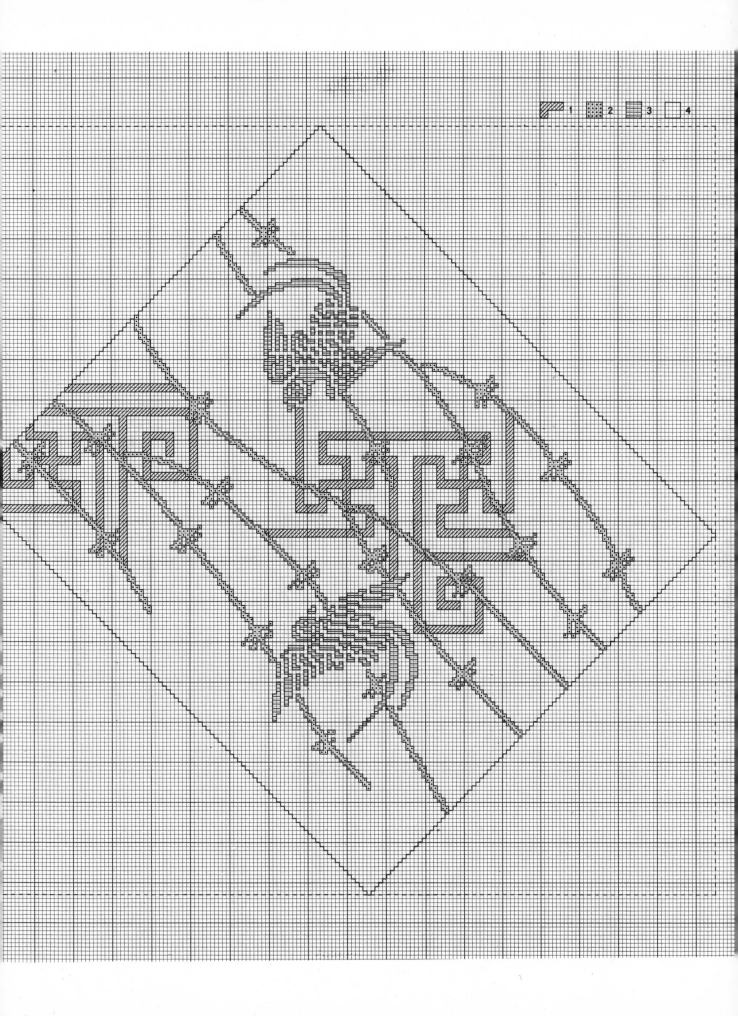

24. Summer Grasses on Lightning-Bolt Lattice, Cushion 18½″ x 15″

This design comes from an eighteenth-century *chō-ken* jacket, woven in gold brocade *(kinran)* on a figured gauze-weave silk ground.

CANVAS: 10 mesh to the inch. Oval design is set on the diagonal within a square 178 mesh by 178 mesh, about 18″ by 18″. Center the design within a square of canvas at least 20″ by 20″. The extra blocking procedure described on page 11 will not be necessary because of the compensating nature of the background stitch; block as usual, following the lines of the square in which the design is set.

NEEDLE: #18.

STITCHES: Basic Stitch for main design; to work background lattice pattern, see STITCHES, Diagram 4, page 16.

YARNS: Bucilla Spotlight gold-tone metallic yarn, 20-gram skeins (.7 oz., or about 130 yd.); use strand doubled over, ends anchored (see YARNS):

1) about ½ skein

DMC cotton floss, Article #117, 8-meter skeins (8.7 yd.); use full six-thread strand doubled over to make twelve threads, ends anchored (see YARNS):

2) 21 skeins #367 (medium bottle green)

Persian yarn, using full three-thread strand, or tapestry yarn:

3) 100 yd. (about 2½ oz.) green to match as closely as possible #2 above (such as Bucilla #7, DMC "Floralia" or Laine Colbert #7320, Bon Pasteur Laine Colbert #876, Columbia-Minerva #520, or Brunswick #18).

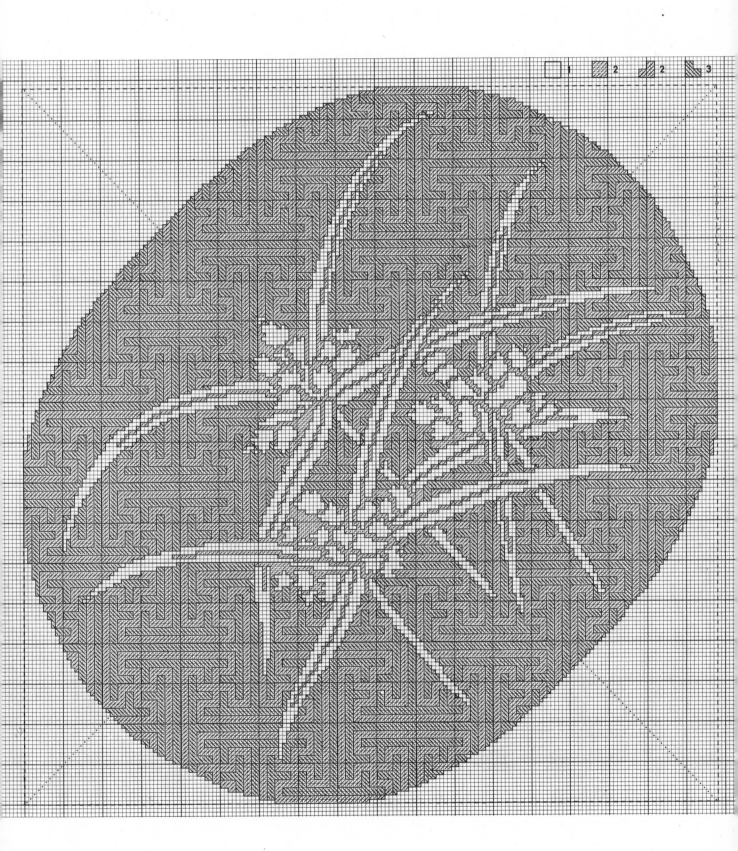

25. and 26. Dandelions on Lightning-Bolt Lattice, Cushions Each 14" x 10" OVAL

The original seventeenth-century *nuihaku* robe was embroidered with dandelions, symbolizing early spring, along with "snow disk" medallions enclosing flowers and grasses of the other seasons as well. The lightning-bolt lattice *(saya-gata)* was originally applied with gold foil on a satin-weave silk ground.

CANVAS: 14 mesh to the inch. Each oval design is set on the diagonal within a square 187 mesh by 187 mesh, about 13½" by 13½". Center each design within a square of canvas at least 15½" by 15½". The extra blocking procedure described on page 12 will not be necessary because of the compensating nature of the background stitch; block as usual, following the lines of the square in which the design is set.

NEEDLE: #22.

STITCHES: Basic Stitch for main design; to work background lattice pattern, see STITCHES, Diagram 4, page 16.

YARNS: DMC cotton floss, Article #117, 8-meter skeins (8.7 yd.); use six threads (see YARNS):

1) *Each cushion:* 2 skeins #783 (bright antique gold)

2) *Each cushion:* 7 skeins #356 (medium rosy rust)

3) *Each cushion:* 7 skeins #922 (terra-cotta)

Médicis crewel yarn, 50-gram skeins; use four strands held together:

4) *Cushion 28:* 7 grams #502 bis (antique white) *Cushion 29:* 4½ grams of the same

5) *Each cushion:* 4½ grams #305 (chartreuse)

6) *Cushion 28:* 4½ grams #415 (deep pine green) *Cushion 29:* 7 grams of the same

7) *Each cushion:* 2 grams #304 bis (light gold).

27. Autumn Flowers on Checked Ground, Fire Screen 17″ x 17″

An arrangement of chrysanthemums, Chinese bell-flowers (kikyo), and grasses, wrapped in paper and tied with a silken cord, and set on a rich, yet subtle, ground pattern, is meant to convey the opulence of garden flowers on a late-autumn afternoon. The original eighteenth-century robe featured this motif, repeated, with variations in the placement of colors, on alternating predominately dark and light grounds. This plan, called katamigawari (half body change), was used frequently by Nishijin weavers for their karaori (Chinese weave) silk brocades. By the use of tiny strips of pure gold leaf lacquered to mulberry-bark paper and woven into the pattern (kinran), karaori brocades emulated the effect of nuihaku, the elaborate embroidery on gold- or silver-foil grounds forbidden for a time by sumptuary laws.

CANVAS: 14 mesh to the inch. Designs covers a 240-mesh square; a square of canvas 21″ by 21″ will be sufficient, allowing a 2-inch margin all around for ease in mounting.

NEEDLE: #22.

STITCHES: Basic Stitch for main design; Scotch Stitch for ground pattern (see STITCHES, Diagram 6, left, page 17).

YARNS: Persian yarn; separate the strand to use two threads:

1) 3 oz. ecru or antique white, to match as closely as possible color #2

DMC cotton floss, Article #117, 8-meter skeins (8.7 yd.); use six threads (see YARNS):

2) 20 skeins Ecru
3) 4 skeins #947 (tangerine)
4) 2 skeins #356 (medium rosy rust)
5) 3 skeins #744 (light maize)
6) 3 skeins #783 (bright antique gold)
7) 2 skeins #334 (medium sky blue)
8) 1 skein #553 (medium lilac)
9) 2 skeins #367 (medium jade green).

NOTE: The design as given fits the 16-inch-square opening of an 18-inch-square fire screen manufactured by Schott Furniture Company of Hanover, Pennsylvania. However, the background area of this design can be increased to accommodate such Williamsburg-style fire screens of larger sizes; simply add another square or two of Scotch Stitch all around.

The accompanying alphabet and numerals graph can be used to construct one's own dated monogram in place of Sue's, as given in the lower right quarter graph of the design. Letters and numerals should be worked in Basic Stitch with Persian yarn, first in the usual direction—lower left to upper right—then in the opposite direction—lower right to upper left—to form Cross Stitch, so that the monogram will be prominent on its rectangular ground worked in Basic Stitch with Ecru cotton floss.

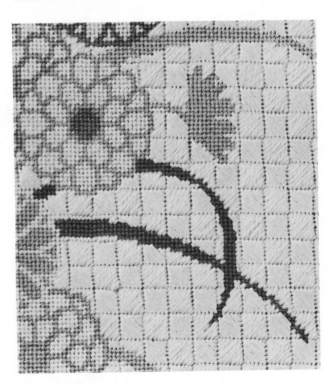

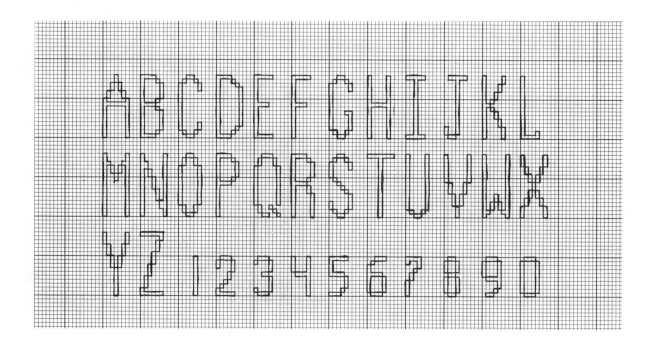

1 2 3 4 5 6 7 8 9

28. Chrysanthemums within a Fence, Cushion 16″ x 16″ ROUND

The original seventeenth-century *karaori* robe featured this design repeated many times as medallions on a lattice ground, which in its turn was a derivation of a Kamakura period (1185–1392) motif used for mirror backs and lacquers.

CANVAS: 14 mesh to the inch. Round design covers 220 mesh by 220 mesh at its widest points; a piece of canvas 18″ by 18″ will be sufficient.

NEEDLE: #22.

STITCHES: Basic Stitch, except for fence areas, which should be worked in Encroaching Gobelin (see STITCHES, Diagram 7, top, page 17.)

YARNS: Fawcett 10/2 linen yarn, 15-yd. skeins:
1) 4 skeins "Gold"

Médicis crewel yarn, 50-gram skeins; use four strands held together:
2) 5 grams blanc
3) 11 grams #419 (medium-light fern green)
4) 10 grams #103 (bright red)
5) 10 grams #415 (deep pine green)
6) 5 grams #124 bis (deep plum)
7) 75 grams (1½ skeins) #505 (putty).

29. "Flaming Drum," Wall Hanging 18″ x 18″

An eighteenth-century *atsuita karaori* robe inspired this design of which the principal motif evokes the pattern on the head of the giant drum used in performances of Gagaku, ancient imperial court theater, precursor of Nō. The chrysanthemum motif is said to be auspicious, and the paulownia motif symbolizes nobility.

CANVAS: 14 mesh to the inch. Design covers a 236-mesh square; a square of canvas 22″ by 22″ will be sufficient, allowing 2 inches unworked margin for ease in framing.

NEEDLE: #22.

STITCHES: Basic Stitch, except for bands of mist marked with symbol #2 on the graph, which should be worked in Encroaching Gobelin (see STITCHES, Diagram 7, bottom, page 17.)

YARNS: DMC cotton floss, Article #117, 8-meter skeins (8.7 yd.); use six threads (see YARNS):

1) 6 skeins #783 (bright antique gold)

2) 6 skeins #738 (wheat gold)

Persian yarn; separate the strand to use two threads:

3) 30 yd. oyster white (such as Bucilla #125, Paternayan #010, Columbia-Minerva #012, or Brunswick #227)

4) 55 yd. medium-light seafoam blue (such as Bucilla #63, Paternayan #352, Columbia-Minerva #342, or Brunswick #185)

5) 20 yd. chartreuse (such as Bucilla #136, Paternayan #Y50, Columbia-Minerva #550, or Brunswick #11)

6) 27 yd. medium olive (such as Bucilla #28, Paternayan #553, Columbia-Minerva #553, or Brunswick #358)

7) 74 yd. brick red (such as Bucilla #51, Paternayan #952, Columbia-Minerva #215, or Brunswick #259)

8) 55 yd. dark brown (such as Bucilla #19, Paternayan #112, Columbia-Minerva #113, or Brunswick #65).

30. Autumn Grasses with Butterflies, Bed Rest

This design comes from a seventeenth-century Nō costume jacket of the type called *chōken* ("long silk"). It is actually a shorter jacket than the *maiginu* (see Design 4), another costume used characteristically as a dance robe for female *shite* in third-category plays. This arrangement of larger motifs across the upper part of the garment with smaller scattered motifs below is typical of *chōken* design, and the classical chrysanthemums within a fence motif (see Design 28) is evoked by the angular, straight-sided basket. The basket and butterflies of the original garment were woven of gold-foiled thread on a purple gauze-weave silk ground. The patina or *sabi* of age acquired by such a garment confers great value and distinction.

CANVAS: 14 mesh to the inch.
NEEDLE: #20.
STITCH: Basic Stitch.

IMPORTANT NOTE: For cutting diagram and total amount of canvas required, see page 18.

YARNS: Bucilla Spotlight gold-tone metallic yarn, 20-gram skeins (.7 oz., or about 130 yd.); use single strand:
1) 2 skeins
Médicis crewel yarn, 50-gram skeins; use four strands held together:
2) 4 grams #411 (medium-light fern green)
3) 3 grams #407 (medium jade green)
4) 3 grams #128 (coral)
5) 1½ grams #103 bis (light pink)
6) 2 grams #210 (light blue)
7) 12 skeins #409 (deep blue green).

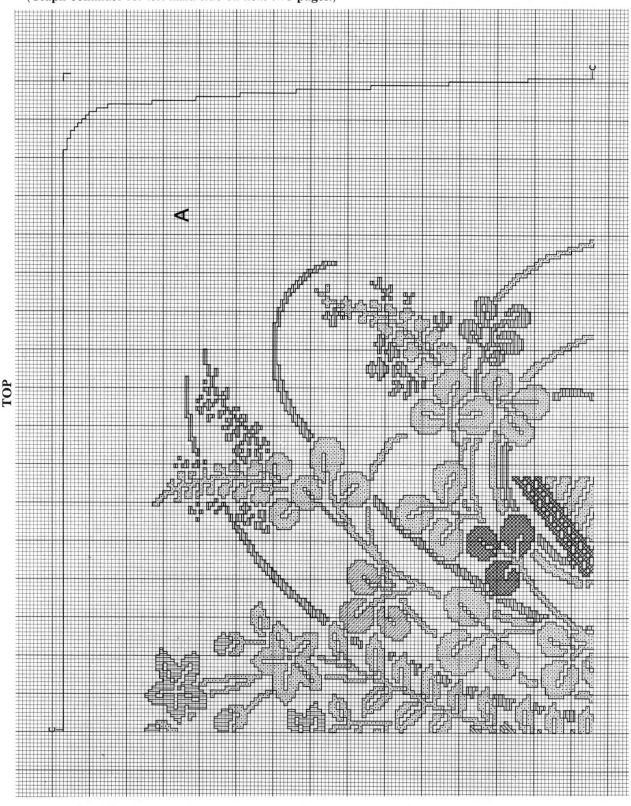

TOP

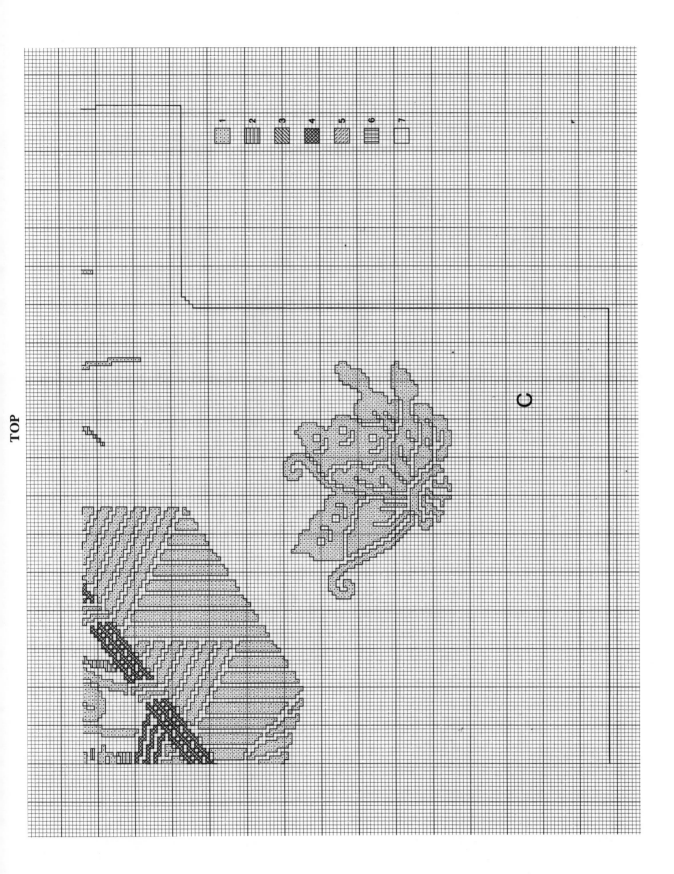

C

TOP

B

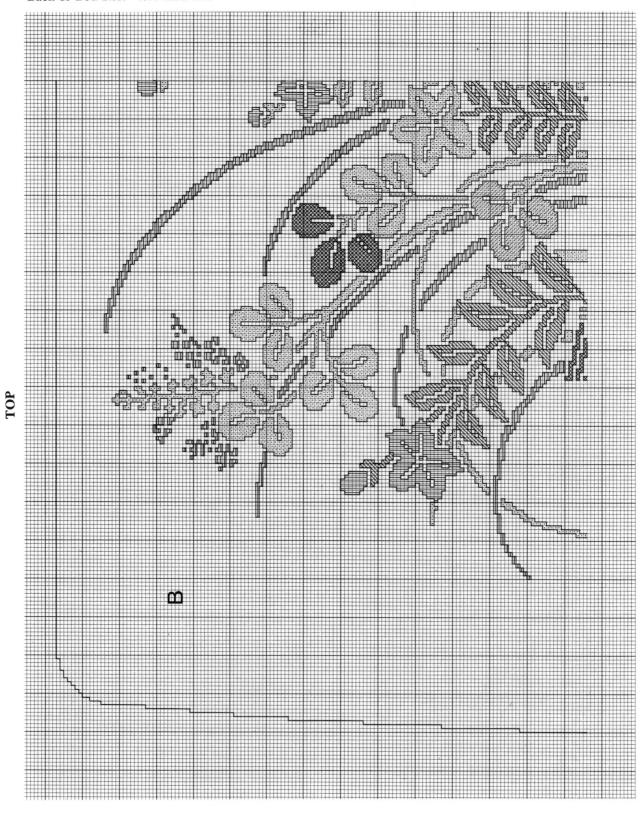

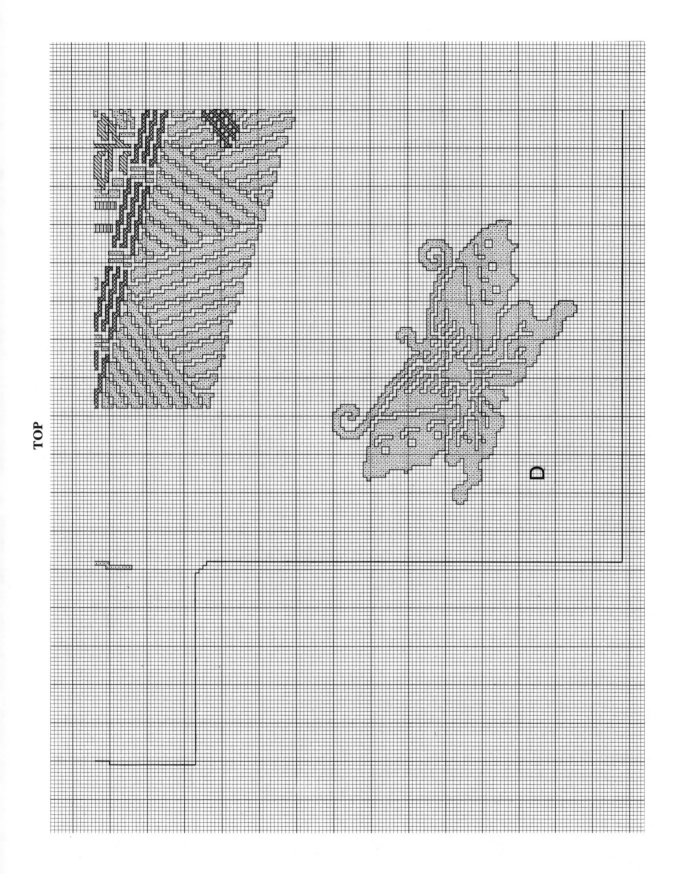

TOP

D

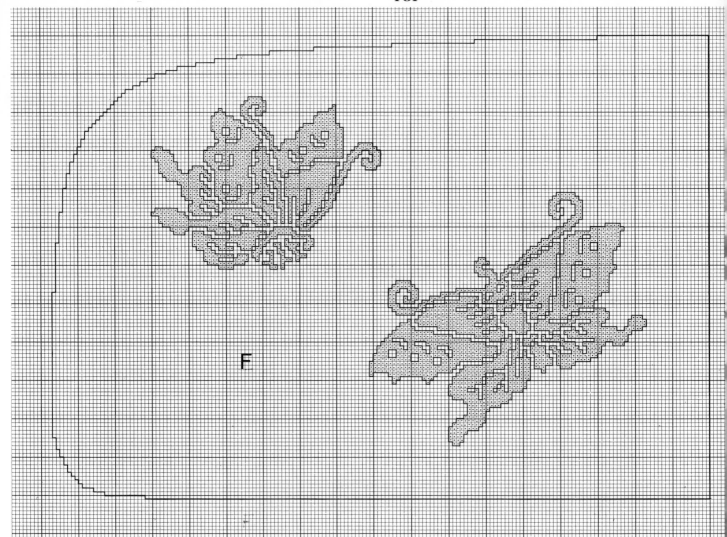

Right Arm of Bed Rest—inside

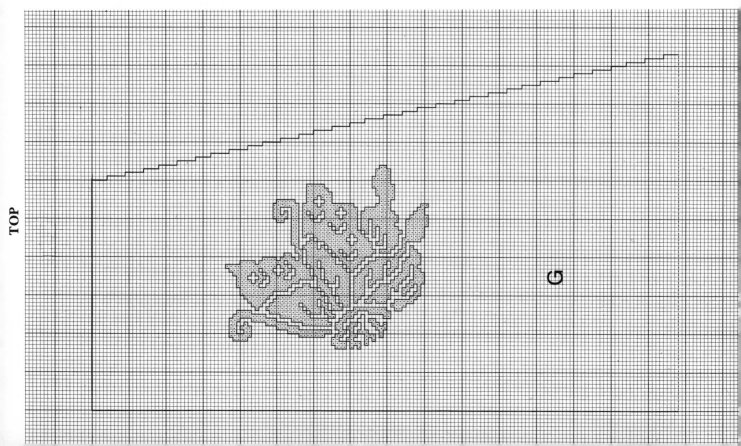

TOP

Right Arm of Bed Rest—outside;
graph begins above.

L

K

TOP

Left Arm of Bed Rest—outside;
graph begins above.

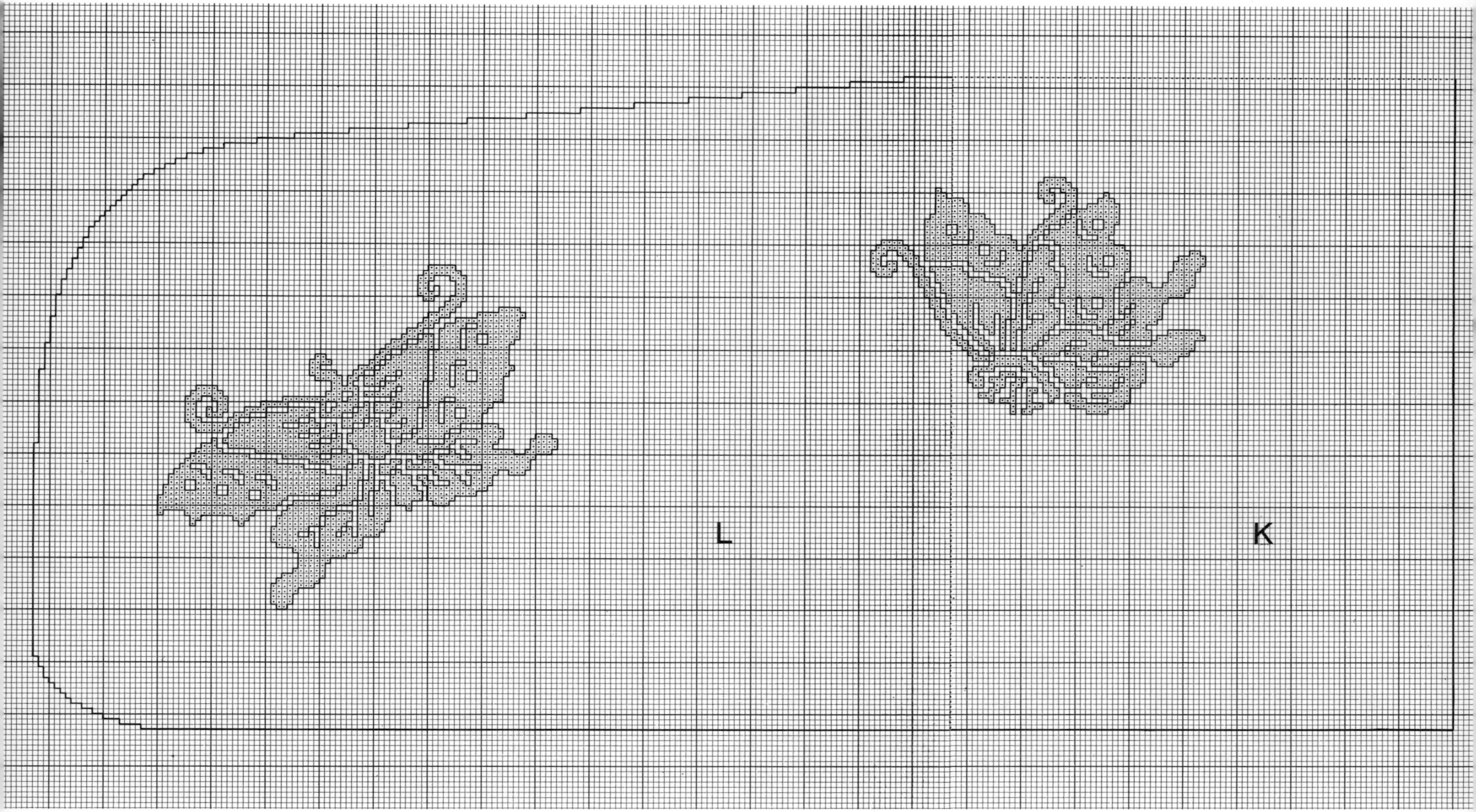

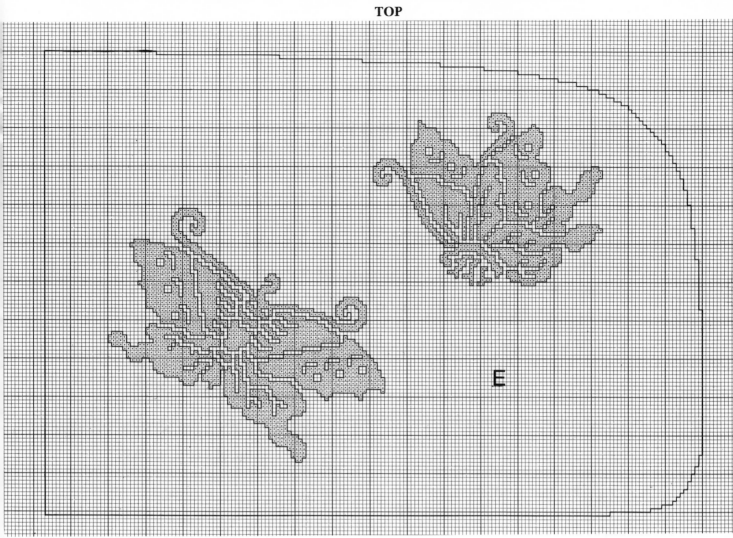

Left Arm of Bed Rest—inside

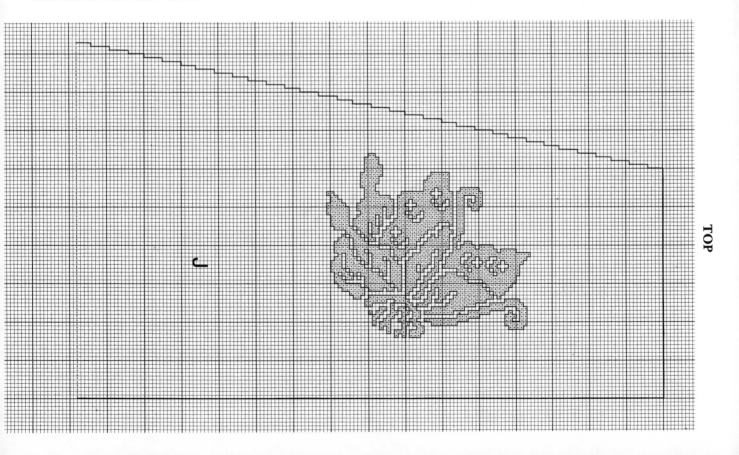

Sources

Bucilla Yarns, 150 Meadowland Parkway, Secaucus, New Jersey 07094.

Frank A. Edmunds & Co., Inc., 6111 South Sayre Avenue, Chicago, Illinois 60608.

Empire Wood Carving Company, Inc., 1640 West Walnut Street, Chicago, Illinois 60612.

Folklorico, P.O. Box 625, Palo Alto, California 94302.

Handwork Tapestries, Inc., 114B Allen Boulevard, Farmingdale, New York 11735 (distributors of Bon Pasteur and Médicis yarns).

Jacmore Needlecraft, Inc., 36 West 25th Street, New York, New York 10010.

Leatherpoint Creations, Inc., P.O. Box 171, West Bend, Wisconsin 53095.

Mark Distributors, Inc., 20825 Prairie Street, Chatsworth, California 91311.

Nantucket Needleworks, Inc., 11 South Water Street, Nantucket Island, Massachusetts 02554.

Norman's Handmade Reproductions, Norman Jernigan, Route 5, Box 838, Dunn, North Carolina 28334.

Pandora Products, manufactured by Rush A. Bowman & Associates, 3723 Oakley, Memphis, Tennessee 38111.

Paternayan Bros., Inc., 312 East 95th Street, New York, New York 10028.

United Stamped Linens Corp., 319 Grand Street, New York, New York 10002 (distributors of all DMC yarns).

Many of the companies above will fill retail orders; if not, they will be glad to inform you of shops in your area carrying their products.

Notes

1. There are three separate and distinct theatres in Japan: the Nō, or classic drama, with its masked figures, perfected five hundred years ago; *Ningyo-shibai*, or the doll-theater, where marionettes interpret complicated ballad-dramas; and *Kabuki*, the popular theatre. . . . These are the Japanese theatre

arts, interwoven into the very fabric of society, the amusements of the people that reflect their psychology, tastes, and aspirations.

The Nō became crystallized into an art at the time of the Shogun Yoshimitsu (1368–98). Long before Yoshimitsu held sway, the country had been brimful of song, dance, poetry, minstrelsy, and the three theatres of modern Japan may be said to have inherited the accumulated tendencies of a thousand years.

Deeply rooted in the people was the love of theatrical entertainments which were held in connection with the festivals of shrines and temples. From these performances developed companies of players who formed hereditary actor families, the members of which were regarded as belonging to the common people.

When Yoshimitsu saw a performance at a Kyoto temple that pleased him he gave his patronage to the players, and at one bound they were elevated to a new position. It was at this time that the Nō was brought to a state of perfection, and the support and encouragement given by so highly placed a personage resulted in the monopoly of this theatre by the aristocracy, to be reserved henceforward for their own use and entertainment. . . .

—Zoë Kincaid, *Kabuki: The Popular Stage of Japan* (Arno Press, New York, 1971), pp. 5–7.

2. The traditional Nō stage is square in shape, made of highly polished and specially seasoned cypress. . . . Pillars at each corner support an ornate roof which is an integral feature even though today stages are customarily built within an auditorium. This roof has remained a part of the Nō theatre since the days when stages were built out of doors. . . . The pillars serve as direction points for the dancing. On the walls of the recess at the back of the stage a conventional pine tree is always painted; some authorities say this tradition had its origins in the sketch of a pine (the sacred Kasuga-jinga) found in the Kasuga temple at Nara. At the right of this is a small sliding door called the *kirido*, through which the chorus and stage assistants make their entry and exit. There is a ballustraded extension of the stage . . . to the right of the audience, and here the chorus sit. The orchestra sits immediately in front of the painted pine tree in the space known as *atoza*. At the front of the main stage there is a small flight of steps down to the auditorium, now purely ornamental, but a relic of the times when an actor was summoned to speak to high authority. The actors make their entry along the *hashigakari*, a roofed and ballustraded passage which connects the stage platform with the green-room. . . . At the side of the *hashigakari* are planted three small pine trees standing in the pebbled walk which runs the length of the structure and along the front of the main stage. The entrance to the *hashigakari* is covered by a curtain, the *agemaku*. . . . On the inner side of the curtain two poles are attached to the bottom; attendants seize these and lift the curtain high with a swift movement when an actor comes on or goes off the stage. Behind the curtain is a room called the *kagaminoma*, or mirror room, so named because there is a large mirror in front of which the actors adjust their wigs and

costumes and have their masks fixed before making their entry.

The Nō stage is built out into the auditorium so that the audience actually sit on two sides of it; the performance is not seen like a picture in a frame on a single plane, it is a part of the audience. . . .

—A. C. Scott, *The Kabuki Theatre of Japan* (George Allen & Unwin Ltd., London, 1956), p. 49.

3. Noh as an independent and original art form—ultimately destined to supercede the earlier *Dengaku* (field-music), *Sarugaku* (monkey-music) and other song-dances—incorporates the most significant elements of the former and especially of the *Kusemai* (tune dance). With it a new literary form may be said to have been created. The invention of Noh is attributed to Kwannami Kiyotsugu (1333–84), a distinguished actor and writer of *Sarugaku* and to his son Zeami Motokiyo (1363–1443), who developed and refined the art under the patronage of Yoshimitsu, the third Ashikaga shogun. In addition to his dramatic activities, Zeami composed a number of works, the most important of which is called the *Kwadensho* (the Book of the Flower) . . . in which he explained the nature and aesthetic principles governing Noh plays, and gave detailed instructions concerning the manner of composition, acting, direction, and production of these dramas.

The term Noh used substantively to denote "accomplishment," "skill," "talent," derives from a verb signifying "to be able," "to have power," "to accomplish something," and was early applied to actors and dancers. Zeami uses the term to designate that unique type of lyrical drama known as Noh which he subsequently defines as "elegant imitation." In the work mentioned above the author stresses that this form of art consists of two fundamental elements—dance and song. . . . The Noh drama may, in effect, be described also as a lyrico-dramatic tone-poem in which the text has a function somewhat similar to that of the libretto in a Wagner or Debussy opera. The significance of the action, the beauty of the verse, and the excellence of the music and singing, according to Zeami, are purposely designed to "open the ear" of the mind, while the miming (*monomane*) and dancing (*mai*) awaken the emotions of the spectator and "open his eyes" to that supreme form of beauty denoted by the word *yūgen*, which is the ultimate goal and the essential element of all aesthetic expression, be it dramatic or lyrical. The term *yūgen* has no exact equivalent in English; literally it means "obscure and dark," but, as used by Zeami, it carries the connotation of half-revealed or suggested beauty, at once elusive and meaningful, tinged with wistful sadness. Zeami and his successors applied *yūgen* as a critical yardstick not only to works of art but also to the physical appearance and conduct of an individual. Even an old man should, it is said, be represented "like a frowning crag with flowers in its crevices."

—General Introduction to *The Noh Drama: Ten Plays from the Japanese*, selected and translated by the Special Noh Committee, Japanese Classics Translation Committee, Nippon Gakujutsu Shinkōkai (Charles E. Tuttle Company, Rutland, Vermont, and Tokyo, Japan, 1971), pp. ix–x.

4. In his treatises, Zeami lays particular stress on the vital function of miming in the Noh drama, setting down detailed instructions as to its technique which he illustrates by rough drawings. In these each successive movement and posture of the actor is analyzed and worked out in relation to the character of the personage and to the aesthetic effect to be produced. As conceived by Zeami, the mime might perhaps be compared to a continuous, ever-changing series of rhythmic colour patterns woven by the actor with the aid of gorgeous costumes and masks, the ultimate purpose of which is less to please the eye than to serve as a means of creating the *yūgen* mood which is the very essence of the Noh drama.

> —*Ibid.*, p. xiii.

5. The articles of clothing worn, including the many varieties of headgear, reveal the function and dignity of the person. . . . The Nō robes, originally derived from the costumes of the court and military nobility (and the priesthood), were later modified so noticeably that they came to constitute a distinct variety of dress seen only on the stage.

> —Donald Keene, *Nō: The Classical Theatre of Japan* (Kodansha International, Ltd., Tokyo, 1966), p. 66.

6. Around the beginning of the Edo period, the tendency to consider certain patterns and colors absolutely necessary for certain characters began to grow. With further advances in weaving and dyeing techniques, along with the support and patronage Noh received from the government during the Edo period, the unique beauty and refined taste evident in Noh costumes today was developed and formalized. Most of the costumes in use today were made during the Edo period.

> —Yasuo Nakamura, *Noh: The Classical Theater*, Vol. IV, *Performing Arts of Japan* (Walker/Weatherhill, New York and Tokyo, in collaboration with Tankosha, Kyoto, 1971, first published by Tankosha in 1967), p. 213.

7. . . . Noh texts are woven with lines describing, contemplating or enjoying nature. The great importance attached to nature in Noh can be seen by the fact that each Noh has its season or month definitely established. With increasing tendency toward deviation from the long observed practise, the selection of Noh for a program is made, as a rule, according to their seasons as well as other factors. For example, *Kamo*, which is defined as a June Noh, is performed in summer, if not strictly in June. It is with full awareness of the feel of the specific season that Noh is both performed and appreciated.

> —Chifumi Shimazaki, *The Noh, Vol. I: God Noh* (Hinoki Shoten, Tokyo, 1972), p. 22.

8. *Inori* or prayer is a fight between an evil spirit in a woman and monks who try to placate it with prayer. . . . During this dancing action, the serpent woman,

about to cast away an upper garment about her waist, unfolds it. Pulled by a stage assistant, for a moment it forms a triangle before it is dropped. This triangle symbolizes the scale of the serpent, as do the same patterns on the inner garment and the wig band she is wearing. This casting away of the upper garment is called *uroko-otoshi*. . . .

—*Ibid.*, p. 38.

9. Nō, created in the fourteenth century, reached its full growth by the middle of the fifteenth century. It shares much with other forms of expression during the period; it is bare, yet evocative, like the monochrome landscapes; beautiful, yet austere, like the temple gardens; preoccupied with death and the ultimate means of deliverance from life like the literary works inspired by the Buddhism of the time. The movements of the actors owe much to the martial arts that thrived in an age of warfare and to the decorum expected of the Zen priests. The actors' distinctive walk, a bare lifting of the feet from the floor, occurs also in the tea ceremony, another art performed in the fifteenth century. These arts are all marked by an economy of means used to achieve a maximum effect, a preference for suggestion rather than representation.

Suggestion, achieved through the most restrained means, is not an end in itself; like every aspect of Nō it is intended to achieve beauty. . . . But even beauty is not the final object. Nō reaches out towards eternity through beauty and the elimination of the temporal and the accidental.

The Nō plays are set in the distant past and no attempt is made to give them immediacy.

—Keene, *op. cit.*, p. 17.

Bibliography

Design

ARAKAWA, HIROKAZU, and others, *Traditions in Japanese Design, vol. 1, Kachō: Bird and Flower Motifs*, Kodansha International Ltd., Tokyo and Palo Alto, 1967.

GUNSAULUS, HELEN C., *Japanese Textiles*, privately printed for the Japan Society of New York, 1941.

———, "Nō Costume and Mask," *Bulletin of the Art Institute of Chicago*, vol. XXX, No. 6 (November 1936).

KAHLENBERG, MARY HUNT, *Japanese Textiles of the Edo Period,* brochure for the 1970 exhibition, Los Angeles County Museum of Art.

LEE, SHERMAN E., "Noh: Masks and Robe," *Bulletin of the Cleveland Museum of Art,* vol. LXII, No. 2 (February 1975).

——, *Japanese Decorative Style,* Icon Editions, Harper & Row, New York, 1972.

MINNICH, HELEN B., *Japanese Costume,* Charles E. Tuttle Co., Rutland, Vermont, and Tokyo, Japan, 1963.

MIZOGUCHI, SABURO, *Arts of Japan, vol. 1, Design Motifs,* John Weatherhill, Inc., New York, and Shibundō, Tokyo, 1973.

NOMA, SEIROKU, *Japanese Costume and Textile Arts, The Heibonsha Survey of Japanese Art,* vol. 16, John Weatherhill, Inc., New York, and Heibonsha, Tokyo, 1974.

ŌKOCHI, SADAO, *The Tokugawa Collection: Nō Robes and Masks,* catalog for the 1977 exhibition, Japan Society, New York.

PRIEST, ALAN, *Japanese Costume,* catalog for the 1935 exhibition, Metropolitan Museum of Art, New York.

YAMANOBE, TOMOYUKI, *Arts and Crafts of Japan, No. 2: Textiles,* Charles E. Tuttle Co., Rutland, Vermont, and Tokyo, Japan, 1957.

Literature

BOWERS, FAUBION, *Japanese Theatre,* Hermitage House, New York, 1952.

DAIJI, MARUOKA, and TATSUO, YOSHIKOSHI, *Noh,* translated by Don Kenny, Hoikusha Publishing Co., Osaka, 1977.

ERNST, EARLE, *Three Japanese Plays from the Traditional Theatre,* Oxford University Press, London, 1959.

IMMOOS, THOMAS, *Japanese Theatre,* Rizzoli International Publications, New York, 1977.

KEENE, DONALD, *Nō: The Classical Theatre of Japan,* Kodansha International Ltd., Japan, 1966.

KINCAID, ZOË, *Kabuki: The Popular Stage of Japan,* Arno Press, New York, 1971 (first published in 1925 by the Macmillan Company).

LOMBARD, FRANK ALANSON, *An Outline History of the Japanese Drama,* Haskell House, New York, 1966.

NAKAMURA, YASUO, *Noh: The Classical Theater, Performing Arts of Japan,* vol. 4, Walker/Weatherhill, New York and Tokyo, in collaboration with Tankosha, Kyoto, 1971 (first published by Tankosha in 1967).

NIPPON GAKUJITSU SHINKŌKAI, *The Noh Drama: Ten Plays from the Japanese,* selected and translated by the Special Noh Committee, Japanese Classics Translation Committee, N.G.S. (The Japanese Society for the Promotion of Science), Charles E. Tuttle Company, Rutland, Vermont, and Tokyo, Japan, 1971 (first published in 1955).

ORTOLANI, BENITO, *Zenchiku's Aesthetics of the Nō Theatre,* Riverdale Center for Religious Research, The Bronx, New York, 1976.

POUND, EZRA, and FENOLLOSA, ERNEST, *The Classic Noh Theatre of Japan,* New Directions Publishing Corporation, New York, 1959 (first published in the U.S.A. in 1917 by Alfred A. Knopf, Inc., as *"Noh" or Accomplishment, a Study* of the Classical Stage of Japan).

SCOTT, A. C., *The Kabuki Theatre of Japan*, George Allen & Unwin Ltd., London, 1956.

SHIMAZAKI, CHIFUMI, *The Noh, vol. I: God Noh*, Hinoki Shoten, Tokyo, 1972.

——, *The Noh, vol. III: Woman Noh 1*, Hinoki Shoten, Tokyo, 1976.

TOITA, YASUJI, *Kabuki: The Popular Theater, Performing Arts of Japan*, vol. 2, Weatherhill/Tankosha, New York, Tokyo, and Kyoto, 1974 (first published by Tankosha in 1967).

WALEY, ARTHUR, *The Nō Plays of Japan*, Grove Press, Inc., New York (first published in 1920).

My Special Thanks

We wish to thank Mr. and Mrs. Goran Holmquist
for permitting us to photograph
some of the designs at their summer home in Maine . . .

. . . and for so beautifully executing the designs:

Mary E. Adams, Brunswick, Maine
Diane E. Baxter, Brunswick, Maine
Mary Beals, Waterville, Maine
Desneige Bernier, Pejepscot, Maine
Jane C. Bowers, Brunswick, Maine
Nancy C. Carter, Falmouth, Maine
Pamelia E. Choate, Winthrop, Maine
Jane Crichton, Brunswick, Maine
Barbara Dana, Cumberland Foreside, Maine
Juanita Fields, Slingerlands, New York
Pamela B. Galvin, Brunswick, Maine
Ann Ward Goffin, Johnson City, Tennessee
Cara J. Hayes, Brunswick, Maine
Jane Hazelton, Topsham, Maine
Jane O. Johnson, Brunswick, Maine
Mieko Maeshiro Korper, Bethesda, Maryland
Judith A. Leaman, Brunswick, Maine
Chris Millar, Brunswick, Maine
Maureen Thomas Osier, Montgomery, Alabama
Marie Palazo, Jamaica Plain, Massachusetts
Petie Palazo, Brunswick, Maine
Bettina M. Piecuch, Belgrade Lakes, Maine
Marion D. Poor, Augusta, Maine
Marguerite Rafter, Wiscasset, Maine

Pat Robinson, Brunswick, Maine
Charlotte B. Rose, Brunswick, Maine
Elena Schmidt, Brunswick, Maine
Ebba F. Sonne, Morton Grove, Illinois
Arlene Stack, Manville, New Jersey
Carol Stark, Brunswick, Maine
Selma Sternlieb, Brunswick, Maine
Jane Taboney, Brunswick, Maine
Judith A. Thornton, Brunswick, Maine
Mary Hoffman Treworgy, Brunswick, Maine
Hannah Prescott Vigue, Brunswick, Maine
Susan B. Wheatland, Cumberland Foreside, Maine

for finishing the cushions, etc., so nicely:

Ann May, Brunswick, Maine
Marion Soper, Brunswick, Maine

for such fine upholstering:

L. B. Perkins, Lewiston, Maine

for such prompt and expert framing:

The Artisans, Brunswick, Maine
Curtis Framing, Brunswick, Maine

for excellent color film processing:

Tannery Hill Studios, Topsham, Maine.

DATE DUE

JE 2 6			

DEMCO 38-297